THE
NEW
PAVILIONS

THE
NEW
PAVILIONS

PHILIP JODIDIO

WITH 328 ILLUSTRATIONS

Thames & Hudson

First published in the United Kingdom in 2016
by Thames & Hudson Ltd, 181a High Holborn, London WC1V 7QX

The New Pavilions © 2016 Thames & Hudson Ltd, London

Designed by Lisa Sjukur / April

British Library Cataloguing-in-Publication Data
A catalogue record for this book is available from the British Library

ISBN 978-0-500-34322-7

Printed and bound in China by Imago

To find out about all our publications, please visit **www.thamesandhudson.com.**
There you can subscribe to our e-newsletter, browse or download our current
catalogue, and buy any titles that are in print.

On the cover: (*front*) Snøhetta, Norwegian Wild Reindeer
Pavilion, 2001 (photograph Ketil Jacobsen, www.fotografica.
no, courtesy of Snøhetta); (*back; clockwise from top left*) Arne
Quinze, *Uchronia*, 2006 (photograph Jason Strauss, © Arne
Quinze Studio); Stamberg Aferiat + Associates, Shelter Island
Pavilion, 2010 (© Paul Warchol); Heatherwick Studio, Bombay
Sapphire Distillery, 2014 (© Richard Chivers/VIEW Pictures/age
fotostock); THEVERYMANY, Vaulted Willow, 2014 (photograph
courtesy MARC FOURNES / THEVERYMANY); Ponadto Grupa
Projektowa, Vistula River Beach Pavilion, 2013 (photograph Rafał
Nebelski, courtesy Ponadto); Sou Fujimoto, Serpentine Pavilion,
2013 (© Paul Raftery/age fotostock); DHL Architecture / Bureau
LADA, Archive, 2008 (© Thomas Lenden); SelgasCano, Serpentine
Pavilion, 2015 (photograph © Iwan Baan). Page 2: Matthew
Woodward, Wirra Willa Pavilion, 2013 (© Murray Fredericks).

CONTENTS

PAVILIONS
FOR ALL

A profound sentiment of change pervades so many aspects of contemporary life that it would be odd for architecture to somehow be left behind. An audio-visual, computer-driven world seems to render each new development obsolete at a pace that leaves all but the most breathless in an occasional quandary. Old school or new school? 3G or 4G? 3D printer or bricks-and-mortar? Architecture, of course, 'suffers' from a drawback that does not plague smart phones and big-screen TV. It is almost relentlessly material. It has to stand up for itself and serve a purpose, the result being that it is most often dreadfully heavy and hard to sweep aside. Even when it is bad, it just stays and stays until the right combination of money and power finally gets the better of it. Architects sometimes still dare to dream of buildings that will remain for centuries, creating a testimony to their own genius. Is architecture condemned to be 'out of it', unable to keep up with the times, imposing itself only by its weighty presence? True, methods of design and even construction have taken up the challenge of the 'digital' age, from Rhino 3D software to CNC milling. Design efficiency beckons, but where any large building is concerned, economics and materials demand a solidity that defies rapid change. This may fundamentally be why architecture and fashion are rarely the best of companions.

Contemporary architecture is not only about great new museums and shining towers. There still exists what might be called a 'cutting edge', though a definition that implies a single way of 'slicing' may be inappropriate. Suffice it to say that there is indeed rapid innovation in architecture.

Rather than looking at the more solid incarnations of the architectural imagination, might it not be better to focus on the transient, the wilfully temporary and usually quite modest world of the pavilion? A few pavilions are meant to last, but most serve a purpose for a defined period of time. These structures find themselves in a world of relatively low budgets and ready experimentation.

More than eighty pavilions have been chosen for this volume, for reasons of geography, variety and inventiveness. The image they define of contemporary architecture is far more relevant and revealing than any selection of 'real' buildings might be, because those who design them can afford to play with the rules, using methods that have never been tried before. As might be expected, computer technology plays a significant role in this process, allowing unique forms to be manufactured, stretching the limits of architecture into new territories that will surely go on to have a significant impact on more 'solid' structures.

The definition of the word 'pavilion' is not as clear-cut as it might first seem. In the *Oxford English Dictionary* at least seven usages are cited:

- A building or similar structure used for a specific purpose;
- A building at a cricket ground or other sports ground used for changing and taking refreshments;
- A summerhouse or other decorative building used as a shelter in a park or large garden;
- Used in the names of buildings used for theatrical or other entertainments;
- A detached or semi-detached block at a hospital or other building complex;
- A large tent with a peak and crenelated decorations used at a show or fair;
- A temporary building, stand, or other structure in which items are displayed at a trade exhibition.

The first definition might make most buildings eligible for inclusion in a book about pavilions. Instead, I want to take a number of specific structures and see how they could be divided into categories, forming a kind of alternative definition to that of the estimable *Oxford Dictionary*.

John Pawson, Martyrs
Pavilion, Oxford,
UK, 2009 (right);
Henning Larsen,
Art Pavilion,Videbæk,
Denmark, 2012 (below)

Some pavilions are works of art in the fullest sense of the term, and change our perceptions of what architecture is and does. One example is the structures of the Icelandic-Danish artist Olafur Eliasson, such as his *Den trekantede himmel* (below and pages 76–77) in Aalborg in Denmark, which celebrates a 'triangular sky' by allowing viewers to enter a mirrored construction that reflects both the atmosphere and the structure itself: a faceted, modified vision of the world.

Another is the work of American artist Dan Graham, who, since the 1980s, has experimented with freestanding steel and glass 'pavilions' more concerned with the ambiguities of perception than with the practical purposes usually associated with architecture. His works, such as *Groovy Spiral* (below and pages 70–71), displayed at Frieze London in 2013, occupy and define space in a way that is not frequently practised by sculpture. In a similar vein the Belgian artist and designer Arne Quinze has embarked on a series of large wooden structures seen in such varied locations as Shanghai (*Red Beacon*; opposite and pages 78–79) and Black Rock, Nevada (*Uchronia*; pages 80–81). From an apparently chaotic assemblage of wooden planks he develops sculptures that verge on the organic, their complexity resolving itself into a defined but still abstract form.

Whereas Eliasson, Graham or Quinze approach the concept of the pavilion from their position as artists, some architects have taken a reverse path, using their knowledge of the built environment to make artistic statements. A case in point is Didier Faustino, who trained as an architect in Paris but today defines himself as 'an alchemist, at once an architect, an artist and a writer'. In *Sky is the Limit* (pages 72–73) – built at the edge of the DMZ in Yangyang, South Korea, in 2008 – he elevated two 'tea rooms' using scaffolding. One room is closed, the other open. The intention of this work is clearly to question the line between art and architecture, but it also indirectly confronts the antagonisms of local history and politics.

Olafur Eliasson, *Den trekantede himmel*, Aalborg, Denmark, 2013 (right);
Dan Graham, *Groovy Spiral*, London, UK, 2013 (below)

SHELTER

While some pavilions are ambitious, in terms of concept and the expression of this in its built form, others appear to be more modest, solely providing shelter for passers-by. These include Kevin Erikson's Rope Pavilion (see pages 256–59) and Michel Rojkind's Hybrid Hut (see pages 262–63) for the city of Winnipeg's Winter Warming Huts competition, which called on architects and designers to build shelters along the river, which freezes over the winter. While modest in appearance, being constructed from materials that primarily expound a relationship to nature, these works were made using computer-assisted design and the expertise of structural engineering firms such as Arup. Kengo Kuma takes the complexity of such structures one step further in his project Casa Umbrella (pages 268–69), utilizing the unassuming form of the umbrella to create an experimental space in which users can seek refuge and adapt their environment as necessary. Meanwhile architects such as the American David Benjamin, push these structures into new realms and in his project Hy-Fi Benjamin created a pavilion entirely from farm waste (pages 10 and 264–67).

LEARN

An even higher degree of experimentation combining sophisticated computation and construction methods with the structures of the natural world has given rise to pavilions produced by MIT and the University of Stuttgart. In 2013 Neri Oxman of the Mediated Matter research group at the MIT Media Lab harnessed the potential of the silkworm to create her Silk Pavilion (2013; see pages 124–25). Here, 6,500 silkworms were encouraged to fill in the gaps between silk threads laid on top of the pavilion's surface by a CNC machine, resulting in a highly unusual structure.

At the University of Stuttgart, Achim Menges, an architect and Director of the Institute for Computational Design, has adopted a relatively similar approach to create what he calls 'temporary bionic research pavilions', which are based on such naturally occurring forms as the skeleton of the sea urchin (see pages 118–19). Working with Jan Kippers, head of the Institute of Building Structures and Structural Design (ITKE), also at the university, Menges has explored what he describes as an 'interdisciplinary approach based on the integration of architecture, engineering and biology' that results 'in an extremely efficient building that offers a unique spatial experience at the same time'.

David Benjamin/The Living, Hy-Fi, Long Island City, New York, USA, 2014 (left); Sou Fujimoto, Serpentine Pavilion, London, UK, 2013 (opposite)

Although the pavilions designed at MIT and in Stuttgart cannot be described as 'beautiful' in the usual sense, they do seem to generate forms that are not related to any building known to date, but which are profoundly connected to nature, whose efficiency obviously can provide many useful lessons in architecture. Computer-driven analysis, design and construction succeed in imitating the apparently complex generation of naturally derived models, whereas in the past, 'organic' architecture was a more subjective and esthetic pursuit, usually unrelated to real material efficiency. The projects of Neri Oxman and Achim are small in scale, and their potential influence on larger, more 'permanent' buildings is not yet established, but their pavilions do break new ground, extending the sources and finality of architecture further into the realm of science and computational applications.

GATHER

Pavilions conceived in laboratories by professors may lack some of the public presence of the temporary structures produced by well-known architects in well-known locations. London's Serpentine Gallery has long called on figures including Zaha Hadid, Frank O. Gehry, Alvaro Siza and Rem Koolhaas to conceive its summer pavilions, which it uses for various cultural events amongst other things. The inventive Japanese architect Sou Fujimoto was called on to design the pavilion in 2013 (above and pages 44–47), using little else than 20mm (⅞in) white steel poles erected in a latticework pattern. Fujimoto is known for making work that questions some of the most fundamental aspects of architecture. Here, precisely because he was building a temporary pavilion, he chose to do away with its walls, ceilings and doors. So much of architecture is focused on the reproduction of conventional interpretations of space that Fujimoto's radical approach has caused others to think and perhaps to follow in his footsteps. For the 2012 Serpentine Pavilion, the Swiss architects Herzog & de Meuron worked with the noted Chinese artist Ai Weiwei (pages 22–23). Though in a different mode to Fujimoto, they too questioned the function and presence of the pavilion, digging into the earth and making a seating area whose forms echoed the 'archaeology' of earlier pavilions. The 'roof' of the building was nothing more than a circular pond supported by thin columns that were placed in a pattern prompted by the remains of the work of their prestigious predecessors on the same site. Here again, walls and doors were done away with, summoning forth architecture of a new kind, which also somehow strips buildings back to their skin and bones, and surely also to their ancient origin as shelters.

Zaha Hadid, Mobile
Art Pavilion for
Chanel, various
locations, 2007-14
(right); Shigeru
Ban, Artek
Pavilion, Milan,
Italy, 2007 (below)

Other pavilions intended as meeting spaces similarly challenge how architecture might be perceived. The League of Shadows created in Los Angeles in 2013 to house the graduation ceremony of students from the noted school of architecture SCI-Arc (pages 14–15, 42–43) is a striking example. Its volume was defined by construction methods akin to those used in the making of composite sails for boats – layered and stitched fabric strips that were calculated to cast cooling shadows over its one thousand sitters. The programme for the structure required an 'innovative, technically implementable, and visually remarkable multi-purpose pavilion'. Realized with relatively limited means, the League of Shadows pavilion is an illustration of the 'lightness' that the genre is capable of, in terms not only of structure but also of conceptualization, based on the premise of ephemerality.

EXHIBIT

Pavilions have long been used for exhibition purposes, vaunting the merits of specific products or works of art within public spaces. Zaha Hadid's Mobile Art Pavilion for Chanel (above and pages 146–47), which has found its way to multiple locations around the world, illustrates this definition perfectly. Her flowing lines unite floors, walls and ceilings to form a continuous shape and space in which the virtues of Karl Lagerfeld and the Chanel brand are promoted.

Though market conditions somewhat curtailed the planned itinerant use of this pavilion, it surely served to draw attention to the designers (Lagerfeld and Hadid). Hadid has of course frequently experimented with the flowing continuity of space seen most dramatically in the Chanel Pavilion, but here she was freed of some of the constraints imposed by the size and function of her more permanent works.

The New York-based architectural office LOT-EK has made creative use of shipping containers to provide another transportable pavilion, in this instance for the Puma brand (see pages 150–51). Cantilevered volumes and the bright red of the brand combine in their structure to draw attention to the participation of the sportswear manufacturer in the 2008 Volvo Ocean Race. Though shipping containers might seem frightfully 'ordinary' in their essence, LOT-EK and others such as Shigeru Ban (opposite and pages 142–43) have found them very useful in works such as Ban's Artek pavilion, precisely because they can be easily moved and represent a defined architectural space that does not require the usual armature of construction.

LOOK / LISTEN

The challenge of providing good acoustics within an outdoor space or making a structure that is just as noteworthy as the views it has been built to highlight were both deftly surmounted by the following two examples. Responding to the brief of creating a three-hundred seat space in which to house performances by the Bavarian State Opera, the Austrian architects Coop Himmelb(l)au made the spiky Pavilion 21 MINI Opera Space in Munich in Germany, 2010 (below and pages 190–93). Temporary and transportable, this pavilion also pushed the limits of architectural design.

A structure perhaps less eye-catching from the exterior but no less well conceived in design is the Norwegian Reindeer Pavilion (see pages 184–87), created by the architects Snøhetta in the form of a viewing 'box' from which visitors could watch the local reindeer population in Norway's Dovrefjell National Park. Stark and minimalist on the ouside, the inside is striking by contrast, comprising undulating 'waves' in wood that cover three walls and serve as a seating area.

Coop Himmelb(l)au,
Pavilion 21 MINI
Opera Space,
Munich, Germany,
2010 (right);
P-A-T-T-E-R-N-S,
League of Shadows,
Los Angeles, USA,
2013 (overleaf)

A pavilion need not be a temporary structure. Indeed there are many good examples that have been built to function as offices (though some, such as Shigeru Ban's Temporary Paper Studio, see pages 232–33, and Rotor's RDF181, see pages 226–27, were eventually dismantled) or as spaces in which to live or play. A good example of this more permanent form of architecture is Shelter Island Pavilion (below, and pages 204–07), built in 2010 by Stamberg Aferiat + Associates as a retreat for their own use on Shelter Island in Long Island, New York. Formed essentially of two 'pavilions' the 102m² (1,100ft²) structure is modest in size, but has been carefully conceived, with the architects drawing on Newtonian colour theory for its palette and the work of Mies van de Rohe, Le Corbusier and Marcel Breuer for its form.

The Harvest Pavilion (see pages 18–19, 228–31) in Kunshan in China, by Vector Architects, is another interesting example for several reasons. The first of a number of small pavilions planned for construction within an 'eco-farm', the Harvest Pavilion, as its name implies, is a space in which crops can be gathered. Elegant and light, it illustrates a variety of pavilion types.

Another essentially permanent building, the Vertical Glass House (opposite and pages 200–03) in Shanghai in China, was originally designed as a temporary building in 1992 and only rebuilt by the West Bund Biennale of Architecture and Contemporary Art very recently. With this work, the architect Yung Ho Chang literally upends a Modernist icon, replacing glass surfaces with concrete and vice-versa – here the floors and ceiling are made of glass, which pokes out through the rough concrete envelope at each of its four levels. Used as a guesthouse for the Biennale, the Vertical Glass House was temporary but became permanent, and is a fascinating commentary on the pavilion as a type of building.

Other examples include follies (the concept of which is almost as difficult to define as that of the pavilion), which from the eighteenth century and beyond have been largely purposeless structures that populate the grand gardens of England and France. A number of contemporary architects have tried their hand at this genre, including the venerable Chinese-American architect I. M. Pei (see pages 216–17), who crafted a garden pavilion for Oare House in Wiltshire in the UK in 2003. Pavilions of a sheltering or religious kind are frequent fixtures of the traditional architecture of Asia, so there is poetic justice in

Stamberg Aferiat + Associates, ShelterIsland Pavilion,Long Island City, New York, USA, 2010

Atelier FCJZ,
Vertical Glass
House, Shanghai,
China, 2013

Pei bringing his own brand of Modernism to the elegant gardens of Henry Keswick, owner of Jardine Matheson Holdings, which has many businesses in China.

These few examples, drawn from the contents of this book, may suffice in order to understand the variety of structures that can be considered pavilions. In these pages they are organized by their primary function or purpose – places in which to gather, seek shelter, work, live or play, learn, exhibition spaces or as objects d'art in their own right. Such is the multifaceted nature of the pavilions selected many could be equally at home in any one of these categories.

The popularity of the pavilion is surely a sign of the times. Often ephemeral and orientated to a specific function, pavilions are also usually less expensive than their more permanent architectural cousins, undoubtedly allowing for more experimentation or inventiveness than larger structures. The pavilion is the architectural form of the moment, and a building type that allows emerging architects to make their mark.

Vector Architects,
Harvest Pavilion,
Kunshan, China, 2012

PAVILIONS FOR ALL

GATHER

KENSINGTON GARDENS
LONDON, UK

ARCHITECTS:
HERZOG & DE MEURON / AI WEIWEI

Jacques Herzog and Pierre de Meuron hardly need to be introduced. Both born in Basel in 1950, they founded their partnership in 1978, and in 2001 were winners of the prestigious Pritkzer Architecture Prize. In 2012 they were called on to design the summer pavilion for the Serpentine Gallery, and collaborated with the Chinese artist Ai Weiwei to work on the concept. Unlike the more exuberant pavilions that had been previously produced at the site, the Swiss pair chose to create a simple steel disk, 10m (394in) diameter, and elevated just 1m (39in) above ground level, with a cork-clad seating area installed beneath. Of their proposal, the architects explained that it was their intention to 'instinctively...sidestep the unavoidable problem of creating an object, a concrete shape'. Nonetheless, their structure incorporated pavilions whose aim may have been exactly that: on digging 1.5m (60in) down, they stumbled across the foundations of other architects' designs for the site, overlapping like a 'jumble of convoluted lines'. Eleven of the twelve load-bearing supports in their pavilion corresponded to such foundations. Of the structure they explained, 'The roof resembles that of an archaeological site. It floats a few feet above the grass of the park, so that everyone visiting can see the water on it, its surface reflecting the infinitely varied, atmospheric skies of London. For special events, the water can be drained off the roof as from a bathtub, from whence it flows back into the waterhole, the deepest point in the pavilion landscape. The dry roof can then be used as a dance floor or simply as a platform suspended above the park.' The steel magnate Lakshmi Mittal purchased the pavilion for his own collection after it closed to the public on 14 October 2012.

The cork-clad seating
(above, opposite
below) of the
pavilion refers
to the 'archaeology'
of the site. The
'floating' roof
(opposite top),
which collects water
for circulation
within the structure.

PARC DES RIVES
YVERDON-LES-BAINS, SWITZERLAND

ARCHITECT:
LOCALARCHITECTURE

Each of the pavilions
was positioned to
highlight the
boundaries of the
park, leaving a
large empty space
at its centre for
recreational use.

In 2007 the municipality of Yverdon-les-Bains commissioned Localarchitecture and the landscape designers Paysagestion to create a public park next to the lake of Neuchâtel, in an area that had formerly been marshland. In addition to the provision of large open green spaces and sports facilities, the park programme called for a small bar and restaurant, picnic shelters, a pedal-boat rental area, a music kiosk and a meditation kiosk. The pavilions conceived by Localarchitecture were intended to highlight the relationship between the canals that ran either side of the site and the newly created park itself, with the structures being dotted along or close to promenades facing onto the water. The post-and-beam buildings were made using braced wooden planks, incorporating single-slope roofs and seating areas as required. The pavilions were also lit at night, a feature that made them resemble 'little lanterns floating at the water's edge'.

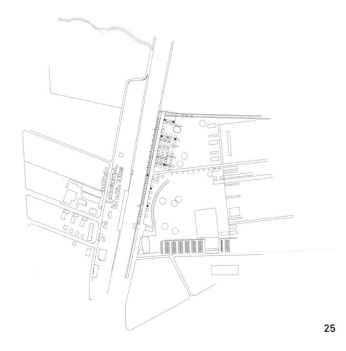

**POTTERS FIELDS PARK
LONDON, UK**

**ARCHITECT:
DSDHA**

Potters Fields Park is located on the south bank of the river Thames in London, between Tower Bridge and the Foster + Partners-designed City Hall. One of the few remaining open green spaces along the river, the area was renovated in 2007, which included the addition of a number of small pavilions. The client – estate management firm More London Ltd – appointed DSDHA to design two pavilions within the park, to a budget of £600,000 (€824,000). The first, Parkside Pavilion, is positioned next to City Hall and includes space for a café, public conveniences and storage (it also conceals the City Hall's facilities: the vents and a cleaning crane). The second, Blossom Square, was built beside Tower Bridge but demolished in 2012 to make space for a housing development scheme. Both structures were made with horizontally stacked timber but the exterior of each was distinct – Parkside displaying a charred black exterior and Blossom Square a light 'calcified appearance', and a green roof. Of Parkside Pavilion the architects explain, 'The form of the building is derived from an analysis of movement and views on the site. Its carved form is set within a group of trees that create a veiled view of City Hall. The setting relates to a strong English landscape tradition of grottos and groves and attempts to encourage the public to make use of all of the riverside public space the site has to offer.' The use of charred wood also brings to mind Japanese *yakisugi*, a technique that involves the production of burnt timber for use in buildings.

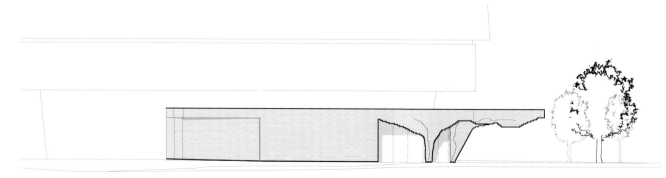

The grotto-like
entrance to Parkside
Pavilion (opposite),
which can also be
seen in plans for
the site (below).
The contemporary
form of Foster +
Partners' City Hall
looms large behind
the more organic
structure (right).

GATHER

Blossom Square, which
was demolished in
2012 to make way
for the One Tower
Bridge development.

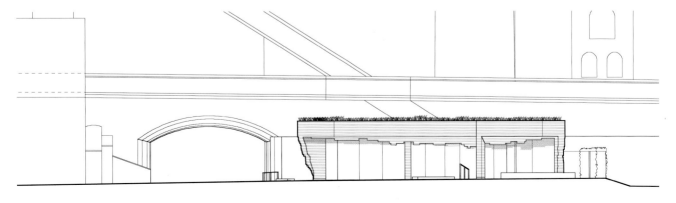

DSDHA

**KENSINGTON GARDENS
LONDON, UK**

**ARCHITECT:
SELGASCANO**

The pavilion designed by Madrid team SelgasCano is a recent addition in a long list of structures that have been created for the Serpentine Gallery in London, which include proposals by SANAA in 2009, Jean Nouvel in 2010, Peter Zumthor in 2011, Herzog & de Meuron and Ai Weiwei in 2012 (pages 22–23) and Sou Fujimoto in 2013 (pages 44–47). SelgasCano's pavilion, which they describe as a 'chrysalis', was made from a double skin of EFTE membrane wrapped in brightly coloured webbing. As the architects explain, 'We sought a way to allow the public to experience architecture through simple elements: structure, light, transparency, shadows, lightness, form, sensitivity, change, surprise, colour and materials. We have therefore designed a Pavilion which incorporates all of these elements. The spatial qualities of the Pavilion only unfold when accessing the structure and being immersed within it. Each entrance allows for a specific journey through the space, characterized by colour, light and irregular shapes with surprising volumes.... At the heart of the Pavilion is an open space for gathering as well as a café.'

A tunnel and the central gathering space within the chrysalis-like structure (opposite). The exterior (above) and the pavilion illuminated at night (overleaf).

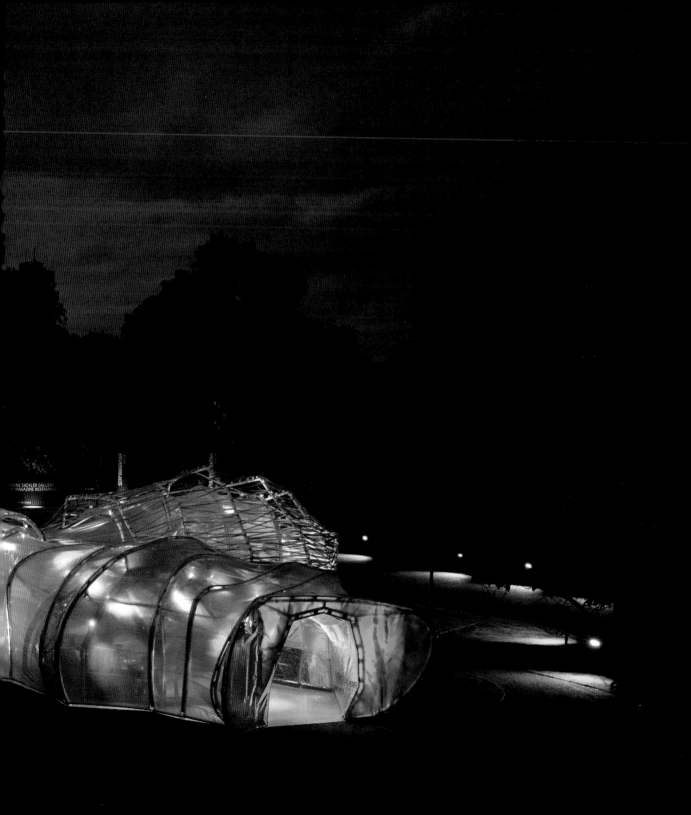

UPCYCLING PAVILION

**EXPO CIHAC
MEXICO CITY, MEXICO**

**ARCHITECT:
BUNKER ARQUITECTURA**

Expo CIHAC is the most significant trade show for the construction industry in Latin America. Approximately five hundred exhibitors present themselves each year at the Centro Banamex exhibition centre in Mexico City, where the show is held. Fairs such as the Expo create vast quantities of waste, with the products exhibited and the stands themselves usually 'ending up in the trash'. Acknowledging this as a principal concern within his design, Estaban Suarez, founder of Bunker Arquitectura, explains, 'we approached the exhibition principals with the proposal of creating a low-cost, zero-waste sustainable pavilion that could set an example for future exhibitions. Inspired by the upcycling movement, which focuses on converting waste materials or useless products into new materials or products of better quality or for better environmental value, we conceived a pavilion made up exclusively of soda crates piled on top of each other.' The structure surely represents good advertising for Coca-Cola, whose crates were used in the design, and who offered not only to lend them to the architects but also to transport them, free of charge. The 300m² (3,229ft²) pavilion was erected especially for Expo CIHAC 2012 and, in keeping with the principles of upcycling, repurposed otherwise useless materials, which have the added advantage of being colourful and easy to stack.

The architects used approximately five thousand Coca-Cola crates in this bright, inexpensive and ecologically responsible design.

NOMIYA

PALAIS DE TOKYO
PARIS, FRANCE

ARTIST / ARCHITECT:
LAURENT GRASSO / PASCAL GRASSO

A project designed by the artist Laurent Grasso, and carried out in collaboration with his brother, the architect Pascal Grasso, Nomiya was a 64m² (690ft²) transportable restaurant pavilion constructed on the rooftop of the Palais de Tokyo in Paris in the spring of 2009. The 18m (59ft)-long structure was partially built in a shipyard in the city of Cherbourg before being assembled in its temporary location. Seating only twelve, the restaurant takes its name from the Japanese word *nomiya*, which means a small bar or restaurant that serves sushi. Related in its form to shipping containers, albeit in a more sophisticated gamut of materials, this glass cabin has a perforated metal screen that encloses the kitchen space, white Corian furniture and a grey, wooden floor. The LED lights positioned at the external periphery of the pavilion and suspended within the dining space give it particular visibility in the evening, corresponding to the spectacular views of the Eiffel Tower and other Paris monuments. The location was, prior to the installation of Nomiya between 2007 and early 2009, the site for the Everland Hotel, a single-room transportable cabin conceived by the artists L/B (Sabina Lang and Daniel Baumann) that was part of Expo '02 in Yverdon in Switzerland in 2002.

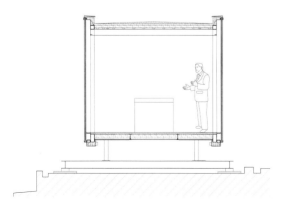

Employing a very
simple structure,
Nomiya offers
spectacular views
of the city from
its rooftop location.

GATHER

The pavilion's
geometric simplicity
is in contrast to the
monumental structure
of the Palais de
Tokyo, which was
built for the 1937
International
Exhibition of Arts
and Technology
(opposite). The
interior (above)
is equally minimalist
in design.

LAURENT GRASSO / PASCAL GRASSO

THE ROOF THAT GOES UP IN SMOKE

ARCHITECT:
OVERTREDERS W

Made up of two picnic tables, a floating 'roof' and
a wood-burning stove, The Roof that Goes Up in Smoke
is a mobile pavilion originally conceived for use as
a meeting space on All Souls Day. The structure is 4m
(13ft) high and can accommodate up to forty people,
and requires only an area of 6 × 9m (20 × 30ft) for its
installation. It is illuminated at night and the inflatable
roof filled with hot air from the stove. The pavilion
can be constructed by a team of only two, takes three
hours to build and can be dismantled in just two. It was
installed in three different locations in the Netherlands
– at graveyards in Roosendaal and Breda and at an
institution for mental health in Biezenmortel – and has
been used at many different festivals and events in the
Netherlands and Belgium since then. The Amsterdam-
based architects Overtreders W (which translates as
Trespassers W) explained, 'When working on the design,
we wanted to create a light and comforting meeting
space to be used in dark and chilly autumn nights,
with a wood fire for people to sit next to and tell stories.
We started experimenting with capturing the hot air
of the wood fire inside an inflatable roof, and lighting
up the roof from the inside. After a few alterations,
these experiments led to the final design.'

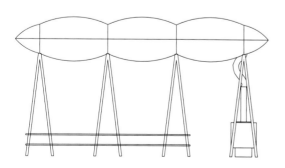

Braces suspending
a hot-air 'pillow'
over picnic tables
are the essential
elements of this
pavilion without
walls — here shown
in its location
in Roosendal.

LOS ANGELES, USA

ARCHITECT:
P-A-T-T-E-R-N-S

The pavilion was on
site for the duration
of one year and
housed events and the
graduation ceremony
for the students and
staff of SCI-Arc.

When designing this pavilion for the purpose of housing the graduation ceremony for students of SCI-Arc (Southern California Institute of Architecture), the architects noted that previous structures built for this purpose had performed only this function, consigned to become 'abandoned vessels' thereafter, devoid of activity. It was the intention of their proposal to avoid this fate, as they explained, 'We believe that if executed correctly, the pavilion could potentially activate a node within the downtown area.' With this as its focus, the League of Shadows pavilion has a dual appearance, forming a 'complex radiating superficial texture at close range' and being a distinctive outline perceivable from a distance. Set at the corner of 4th and Merrick Streets, the structure functions as a public event space and as a 'formal beacon that reasserts SCI-Arc's institutional presence in downtown Los Angeles'. Its vertical form was calculated to provide shelter for up to one thousand people, with its construction process being not unlike that of the production of boat sails, with strips of fabric being layered and sewn together to make large sheets of cloth which, when fixed in place, revealed its final form. Its name references a secret society featured in the Batman movies, but also the shadows it casts, and it was the winner of the 2012 Outdoor Pavilion Competition, organized in the summer of 2012 by SCI-Arc for proposals for an 'innovative, technically implementable, and visually remarkable multi-purpose pavilion'.

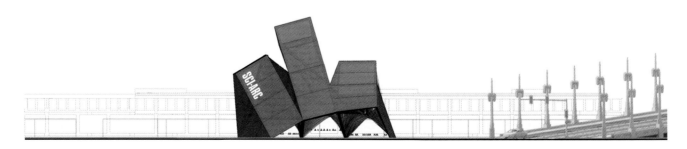

**KENSINGTON GARDENS
LONDON, UK**

**ARCHITECT:
SOU FUJIMOTO**

Since Sou Fujimoto founded his practice in Tokyo in 2000, it has become evident that he is one of the rising talents of Japanese architecture. He is also one of three Japanese architects – after Toyo Ito in 2002 and SANAA in 2009 – to have created a pavilion for the Serpentine Gallery in London. His 2013 proposal involved a 357m² (3,843ft²) structure built using 20mm (1in)-diameter white steel poles, which were positioned into a latticework pattern. The pavilion was designed to be multi-purpose in function: a space that could be used both by the general public and for the events organized by the gallery. Fujimoto has long challenged the conventions of contemporary architecture, questioning the essence of what constitutes a building – or a pavilion in this instance – throughout much of his practice. The summer pavilion, which is graced neither with walls nor a roof, is a typical example of this approach.

As Fujimoto explains, 'It is a really fundamental question how architecture is different from nature, or how architecture could be part of nature, or how they could be merged…what are the boundaries between nature and artificial things.' Clearly, the green setting of the pavilion influenced his design, which, with its semi-transparent, weightless appearance, blends seamlessly into the landscape.

Transparent polycarbonate circles were inserted into the gridwork, to reflect heat and to provide shelter from the rain. So too were squares at various levels, to provide seating for visitors.

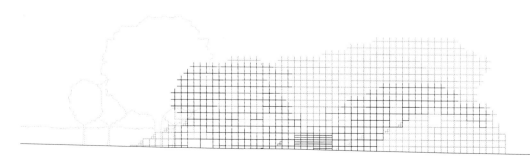

COMMUNITY PAVILION

**THORNTON PARK
NORTH PENRITH, AUSTRALIA**

**ARCHITECT:
MBMO**

The Thornton Pavilion is a 700m² (7,535ft²) structure designed for use as a community centre in a new development area called Thornton Park in North Penrith, near Sydney. According to MBMO director Sven Ollmann, 'The design is a typical pavilion typology, a single-storey building with large glazed façades to the main space leading out onto a terrace and into the landscaped surrounds. The brief,' he explains, 'demanded the challenging combination of openness and security, which was responded to with architectural screens to the outside of the building, which serve as both security screens when the building is not in use, as well as shading devices.' In this instance, MBMO provided full design services based on an existing sketch of the single-storey structure, which includes large, open-plan areas. Although glazed façades are an important part of the design, custom-made perforated 4mm (¼in) aluminium security screens have been employed to offer privacy.

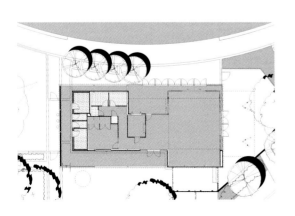

Opened in 2013 as
part of the Thornton
Park development
plan, the pavilion
incorporates offices,
meeting spaces
and amenities for
public use.

WARSAW, POLAND

ARCHITECT:
PONADTO GRUPA PROJEKTOWA

Designed as a space for users of the beach on the Vistula river, and located next to the city's stadium, this pavilion encompasses a café, an area for beach equipment rental, toilets, showers and changing rooms. The $1500m^2$ ($16,145ft^2$) structure, whose predominant materials are wood and concrete, takes the form of two buildings, which are interlinked via a series of ramps, terraces, stairs and public areas. To avoid flooding from the river, the pavilion is elevated above ground by steel posts, with the stairs and ramps linking the street level to the beach. In addition to providing services for the public, the pavilion also houses exhibitions and other small events.

The stairs leading
from street level to
the beach (right),
the north pavilion,
in which the cafe
is housed (opposite
top) and a detail
of the underside
of the steps
(opposite below).

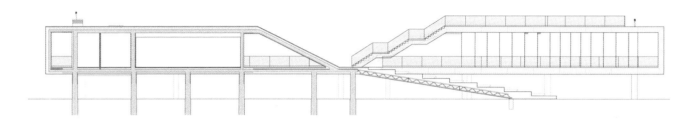

Located in the flood
plain of the Vistula
river, the pavilion
is elevated above
ground by steel pilotis.

FIRE ISLAND PINES PAVILION

FIRE ISLAND PINES
NEW YORK, USA

ARCHITECT:
HWKN

Fire Island is located off the south shore of Long Island and is a popular resort among the gay community. Previously the site for a nightclub that was destroyed by a fire in 2011, HWKN (see also pages 90–91) was commissioned to redesign the building with improved features. Opting for a raw wood structure and a façade made from dynamic triangular frames, the pavilion has a 223m² (2,400ft²) dance floor on the first storey and a 240m² (2,583ft²) terrace, which includes a bar, at ground level. It also has a folding roof so that the club can be opened up during warmer weather. Inside, stadium-style steps 'cascade' down from one wall, providing an elevated view of the dance floor. Centrally situated, the raked pavilion is immediately visible to the 800,000 people who arrive at the island by ferry every summer. HWKN took into account the wishes expressed by residents for a 'sustainable' structure, which is apparent in their extensive use of wood, which is exposed and without excessive cladding, and by their use of a passive cooling system inside. As Matthias Hollwich, co-founder of HWKN explains: 'The building, located at the intersection of all traffic to and from the island, is shaped to become a part of the everyday way of life for the community by fitting in comfortably with the open, beachy and modern feel of the Pines. Going beyond that, we infused every space with a social engine, including the triangular bars that encourage casual meetings, the arena-like bleachers in the nightclub that put the "see and be seen" opportunity into the third dimension, and the inviting openness of the triangular façade frames.'

With its striking asymmetrical structure and criss-crossing timber braces, the pavilion is a key focal point of the resort.

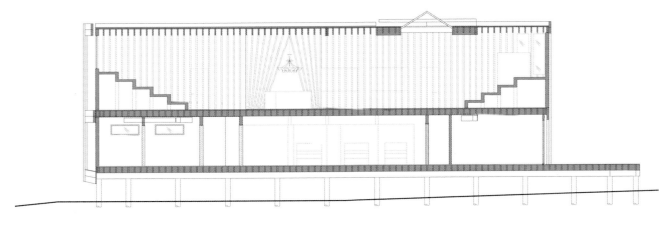

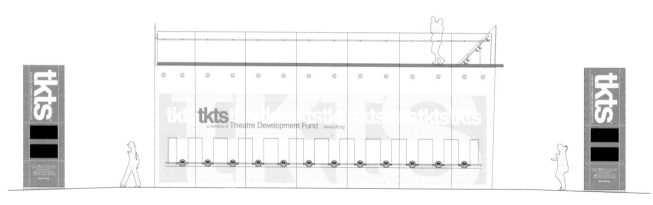

GATHER

**TIMES SQUARE
NEW YORK, USA**

**ARCHITECTS:
PERKINS EASTMAN / CHOI ROPHIA**

This 79m² (850ft²) pavilion was designed as a point of sale for discount tickets to Broadway and off-Broadway shows in New York. Its success as an iconic landmark in Times Square has had a substantial influence on the urban space it inhabits. The project began in 1999 when the Van Alen Institute organized an international competition to redesign the existing TKTS booth. The Australian firm Choi Rophia went beyond the requirements of the brief, imagining the structure as a focal point within the square itself, which included tiered red steps to form an inclined public space. Although Choi Rophia won the competition, the large firm Perkins Eastman was called in to build the structure. The American company introduced a substantial technological element to the design, providing the pavilion with an interior fibreglass shell supported by 8.5m (28ft) glass beams, which made it the largest load-bearing glass building in the world at that time. There is space for up to five hundred on the twenty-seven glass steps, which are lit by LEDs from underneath. A geothermal heating system was introduced to provide air conditioning inside and to keep the steps warm in winter.

The pavilion's
mechanical system
and body was
prefabricated
off-site so that
it could be craned
into position
quickly with minor
disruption to
the area.

The pavilion steps
are made from
triple-laminated
heat-strengthened
glass produced in
Austria. The risers
can be removed to
access and repair
the LED lights.

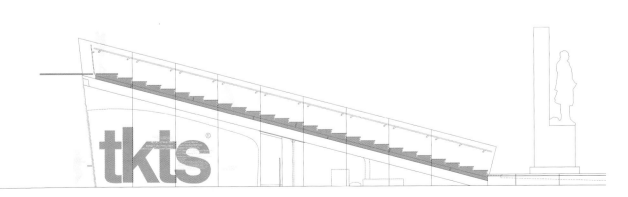

UNStudio's design
was influenced by
another Chicago
landmark: Frank
Lloyd Wright's
Robie House, with
its cantilevered
ceiling and
roof eaves.

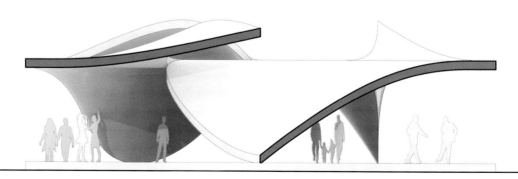

GATHER

BURNHAM PAVILION

MILLENNIUM PARK
CHICAGO, USA

**ARCHITECT:
UNSTUDIO**

Commissioned by the City of Chicago and the Burnham Plan Centennial Committee to celebrate Daniel Burnham's 1909 *Plan of Chicago*, the 300m^2 (3,229ft^2) Burnham Pavilion designed by the Amsterdam firm UNStudio (see also pages 100–01) was made using steel beams and columns, ribbed plywood panelling and elastic plaster (Bondo) and paint. In their design the architects conceived of creating a 'floating and multidirectional space' within the decidedly 'rigid' geometry of the city. An LED system that responded to human activity was integrated into the podium beneath the structure. Conceived by local artist Daniel Sauter, the colour scheme referred to the watercolours that illustrated the *Plan* itself. The design was open on all sides, enabling visitors to view various aspects of the city. With interventions by Zaha Hadid (pages 158–59), Frank Gehry, Renzo Piano and others also in and around Chicago's Millennium Park, this public space gained international significance, while also acknowledging the *Plan* by Burnham as well as some of his early 'modern' architecture, such as the seminal Flatiron Building built in New York in 1902.

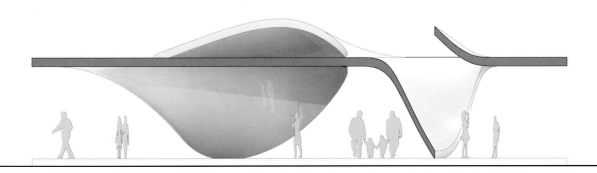

THE LANTERN

SANDNES, NORWAY

ARCHITECTS:
ATELIER OSLO / AWP PARIS

As seen at nightfall, the Lantern glows in the dark, aided by its translucent glass-panelled roof and a lighting system within.

In 2008 the neighbouring cities of Sandnes and Stavanger in Norway, along with Liverpool in the UK, were awarded the status of European capital of culture. It was on this occasion that a programme called 'Norwegian Wood' was launched, a series of design competitions with the aim of promoting 'contemporary, sustainable timber architecture' in Norway. As part of this programme the municipality of Sandnes commissioned a pavilion that could enliven the city's pedestrian area of Langgata, and be used as a place for meeting, markets and performances. Designed by the firms Atelier Oslo and AWP Paris, the 140m^2 (1,507ft^2) structure was built in a small, pedestrianized square at a cost of around £794,000 (€1.1 million). Referencing the traditional wooden houses of the area, it was made using laminated pine boards and steel joints measuring 90 × 90mm (3¾ × 3¾in). Glass panels were mounted directly onto the wood in an overlapping pattern, a departure from the more traditional slate roof typical of the area. The 'sculptural' oak columns that support the structure form benches where they meet the ground. This bringing together of the contemporary and traditional is somewhat echoed in the pavilion's location – there being a contrast between the city square where it resides and the more rural origin of the structures by which it was inspired.

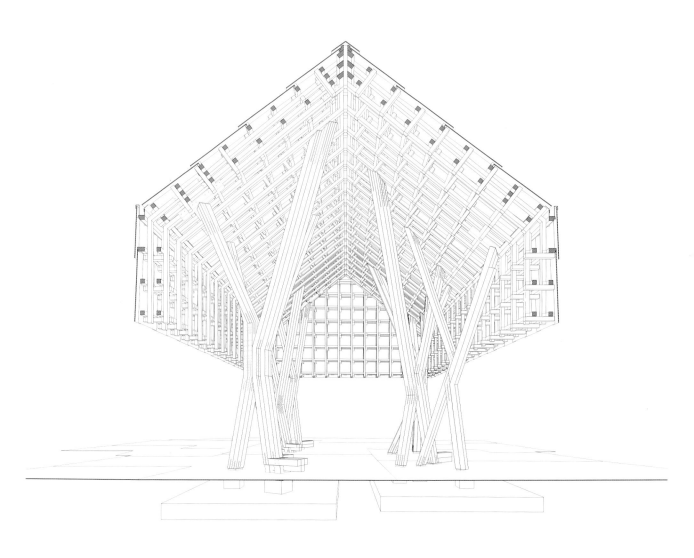

GATHER

The roof is supported by four stilted columns (below, opposite), underneath which is a large space for performances and other activities. The roof was covered in glass-shingles (right) to allow light into the structure.

OSLO, NORWAY

ARCHITECT:
SNØHETTA

Made by Snøhetta (see also pages 184–87) for the purpose of housing the 2011 FIS Nordic World Ski Championships information office, the VM Pavilion was installed on the 7 Juni Plassen in central Oslo. Some of the existing elements of the square were incorporated into the design of this environmentally responsible structure, which was clad with solid oak planks, the intention of which was to bring together traditional Norwegian materials and contemporary architecture. The slate tiles that topped the building were also used for the exterior paving. Inside, the walls were constructed from glulam wooden columns. The light slots in the façades facing the Henrik Ibsen Gate and the Ministry of Foreign Affairs were made from Plexiglas, with fibre optics evoking icicles. The structure itself was formed of two rectangular blocks that were connected by a semi-circular, fully glazed façade facing onto the city's statue of King Haakon. The entire structure was conceived to be easy to assemble, dismantle and remove off site.

The main body of the
structure opens up
onto the courtyard
(opposite top). The
shards of light seen
from the façade refer
to the forms of
icicles (opposite
bottom). The interior
was fitted out with
furniture and
lighting designed
by local firms (above).

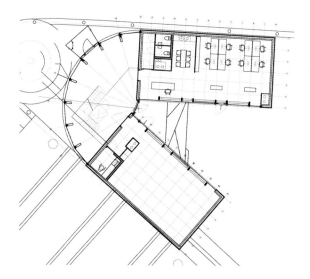

OBJETS

D'ART

GROOVY SPIRAL

FRIEZE LONDON
REGENT'S PARK, LONDON, UK

ARTIST:
DAN GRAHAM

Made from two-way
mirrors supported
by a stainless steel
frame, Groovy Spiral
allowed visitors
views into the
structure, but on
entering the work
they were unable
to see out.

One artist who has consistently referred to the vocabulary of architecture in his work is the American Dan Graham. His installations are typically freestanding, geometric constructs, consisting of steel frames and glass that is either reflective or transparent to varying degrees. Viewers are somewhat disorientated by the intentional reordering of space that he creates with these pieces. Usually, Graham's works fall clearly into the domain of art, since their only discernible purpose is to awaken visitors to just how unreliable their senses can be. One might assume that the purpose of solid, architectural forms is to reassure the user, but Graham's work does the opposite, making them question at every step the space in which they find themselves. And yet the artist often refers to his work as 'pavilions', which surely implies an architectural origin for them. He explains, 'My pavilions derive their meaning from the people who look at themselves and others, and who are being looked at themselves. Without people in them, they might look a bit like minimal-art sculptures, but that's not what they're meant to be.' Exhibited by the Lisson Gallery at Frieze London 2013, *Groovy Spiral* involved the artist's trademark materials of two-way mirrors and stainless steel. Measuring 453 × 731 × 230cm (179 × 288 × 9¾in), the piece was, as Graham explains, conceived to go beyond the rarefied domain of contemporary art: 'What I'm trying to do is deconstruct the corporate two-way mirror – which is the one-way mirror – into something more like a pleasure situation, a kind of heterotopia.'

YANGYANG, SOUTH KOREA

ARTIST:
DIDIER FAUSTINO

Didier Faustino has long been known for his public artworks that have architectural overtones, and which focus in particular on the relationship between the human body and the space it inhabits. In 2002 the artist established the architecture studio Bureau des Mésarchitecture and since 2011 he has been teaching at the Architectural Association School of Architecture in London. In *Sky is the Limit*, he created an unconventional 'tearoom' (in fact two 'rooms', or shipping containers), which were elevated some 20m (66ft) above ground, and could be reached by climbing a five-flight stairwell. The structure was located not far from the DMZ (demilitarized zone) that separates North and South Korea, and the work expresses something of its relationship to this specific site, as Faustino explained in 2015: 'I wanted an atmosphere of antagonism, two opposing situations, which we hoped to show with one open and one closed space. In the end it became a tearoom, something very light that silently reflects on the political issues, which I didn't feel comfortable addressing directly.' The enclosed room offers extensive views of the landscape while the other is open to the wind and rain.

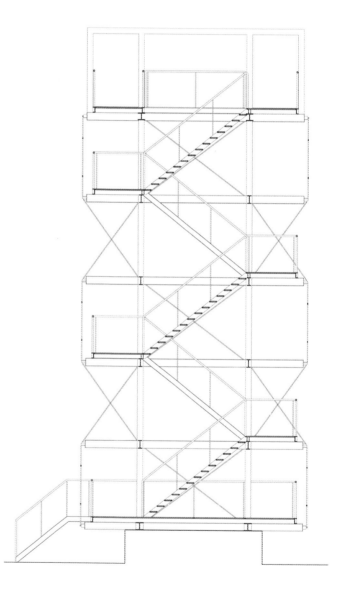

Faustino refers to the body of this structure – comprised essentially from reused shipping containers – as being nothing more than a 'fragile skeleton'.

The pavilion serves
as an observation
deck from which
visitors can reflect
on their immediate
surroundings, as
well as, of course,
on the division of
the two Koreas.

**KUNSTEN MUSEUM OF MODERN ART
AALBORG, DENMARK**

ARTIST:
OLAFUR ELIASSON

Born in Copenhagen in 1967, Olafur Eliasson is one of the most well known contemporary artists working today. Much of his work could best be described as pavilions: *Your rainbow panorama*, a 150m (492ft) circular walkway made from coloured glass panes and situated on top of ARoS Museum in Aarhus (2011); the Harpa Reykjavik Concert Hall and Conference Centre, the façade of which Eliasson created in collaboration with Henning Larsen Architects (2011); and the *Color activity house*, a work made up of three free-standing glass walls tinted in cyan, magenta and yellow, and placed outside the 21st Century Museum of Contemporary Art and City of Kanazawa in Japan (2010), to name just a few. In 2013 he made a piece for Aalborg's Kunsten Museum of Modern Art's sculpture park, to be displayed from 4 May to 25 August. From the exterior *Den trekantede himmel* (*The triangular sky*) is modest in appearance. A trilateral structure supported by three painted V-shaped legs and externally clad in stainless steel, it measures just 364 × 664 × 592cm (143 × 236 × 234in). Inside, however, it is covered entirely in mirrors, providing a multitude of reflections that draws the sky and the immediate surroundings within. As the artist explains, *Den trekantede himmel* 'creates complex kaleidoscopic effects, in which the sky, the surrounding landscape and neighbouring buildings appear in an endless array of fragmented views'. What unites this work, and other architectural pieces by the artist, is how, as spatial interventions, they might affect 'perception, movement, embodied experience and feelings of self'.

Like much of
Eliasson's work,
this mirror-clad
triangular form is
situated at the
juncture between
art and architecture.

RED BEACON

JING'AN SCULPTURE PARK
SHANGHAI, CHINA

ARTIST:
ARNE QUINZE

Some 55 tons of wood were used in the construction of this vibrant red structure, the purpose of which is to encourage social interaction and an engagement with public art.

In 2010 the theme of the World Expo in Shanghai was 'Better City, Better Life', and to coincide with this, the city's Jing'an district organized a public art event, the first of its kind in China, which took the form of a sculpture park. One of a number of works included in the park, Arne Quinze's *Red Beacon* intention was to foster a sort of 'cultural openness in the city' by encouraging the inhabitants of Shanghai to interact with art. The pine board structure was 80m (262ft) long, 30m (98ft) wide and 11m (36ft) high, and painted red. Although both the name and colour of the pavilion might be construed to imply a specific reference to China, Quinze (see also pages 80–81) typically uses orange or red for many structures of this kind. Aside from promoting the field of public art, *Red Beacon* had another goal: 'bringing people back together and generating movement and social interaction' through their use of the structure as a gathering place and shelter.

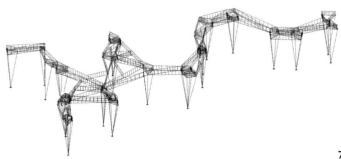

UCHRONIA

ARTIST:
ARNE QUINZE

A wooden, circular construction 60m (197ft) in diameter, *Uchronia* was built for the six-day Burning Man Festival, held annually in Nevada's Black Rock Desert. When the festival was founded by Larry Harvey and Jerry James in San Francisco in 1986, there were only thirty-five participants. In 2006, the year Arne Quinze (see also pages 78–79) created his pavilion, Burning Man had some 69,613 visitors. The event is described by organizers as an experiment in community, radical self-expression and self-reliance and takes its name from the ritual burning of a large wooden structure or effigy on the sixth day. Intended for the 'final burn' or apotheosis of the festival, *Uchronia* was designed with its destruction in mind. Quinze deployed 150km (93 miles) of cedar boards and no less than 350,000 nails in the structure. The artist's firm at the time, Quinze & Milan, had already created similar sculptures on a smaller scale at '100% Design' in London, and fairs at the Design Post Cologne centre. He produced another large-scale wooden sculpture in a similar vein in 2007–08 in Brussels, entitled *Cityscape*. For each of the wooden planks used in the Nevada installation, Quinze had a tree planted in Belgium, for which the ashes from the Nevada 'burn' were used as fertilizer. 'In this way,' he explains, 'we have brought Burning Man to the other side of the world.' The installation included a large sound system and dance parties were held inside every night until its deconstruction. The installation was funded by the Belgian radiator manufacturer Jaga and its CEO Jan Kriekels acted as Art Director for the installation.

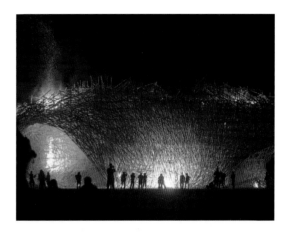

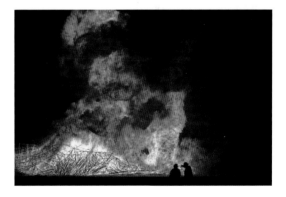

It took a team of twenty-five three weeks to build the sculpture, the sole purpose of which was to be destroyed by fire on the last day of the festival.

ECO EXPERIMENTAL MUSEUM
MEXICO CITY, MEXICO

ARCHITECT:
MMX STUDIO

Every year, the ECO Experimental Museum in Mexico City, created by the artist Matthias Goeritz in 1953, organizes a competition for the design of a temporary pavilion to house events within the main patio of the building. One of a group of museums under the umbrella of the National Autonomous University of Mexico (UNAM), El Eco, as it is called, is devoted to 'temporary contemporary art projects by Mexican and international artists'. MMX Studio, founded in 2009 by Jorge Arvizu, Ignacio del Rio, Emmanuel Ramirez and Diego Ricalde, won first prize for the 2011 competition. The architects state, 'The design does not seek to create a stand-alone piece at the main courtyard; on the contrary, the intervention tries to strengthen the key assets of the original museum, creating an extension of the architectural experiment that the original building pursues.' As opposed to a more solid structure, MMX created a series of interwoven ropes that run above and through two courtyards, 'confining' or enclosing them to some extent, but also encouraging visitors to rediscover the space and the adjacent building. Given its nature, this installation changes continually with the movement of the sun or clouds.

The architects describe this installation as an 'extension' of the museum itself, and its sculptural presence as being defined by natural light.

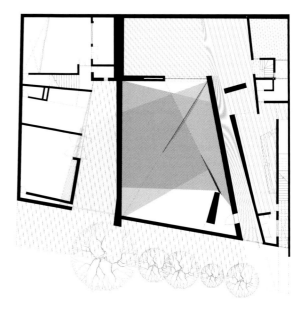

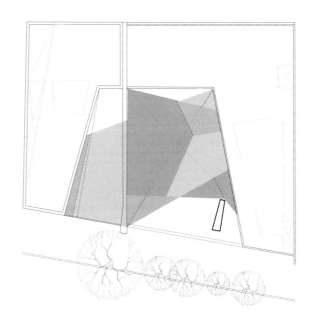

PEACE PAVILION

BETHNAL GREEN GARDENS
LONDON, UK

ARCHITECT:
ATELIER ZÜNDEL CRISTEA

ArchTriumph is a London-based organization that organizes architecture and design competitions to showcase the work of innovative makers in these fields. In 2013 the annual Triumph Pavilion competition was won by Atelier Zündel Cristea (see also pages 222–23) for their Peace Pavilion, a symmetrical self-supporting structure made with 78m² (840ft²) of PVC membrane. Of the proposal they explain, 'To achieve such an apparently complex shape, we used advanced tools of parametric design, the study of tensile membranes and the geometric conception of double-curved surfaces, along with digital fabrication.' The elements required for the structure were made using CNC milling machines and it was built at a cost of around £19,000 (€26,000). The aim of the pavilion was to provide a sense of 'harmony, silence, pureness, kindness, happiness, appeasement, calm, reconciliation, serendipity (and) tranquillity' for its visitors. All of this was achieved by a structure that the architects describe as being essentially 'a simple topological deformation of a torus'. Constructed in Bethnal Green, in London's East End, the Peace Pavilion was an inflatable tube 4m (13ft) high with a clear tensile membrane set on a stainless steel base covering an area of 32m² (344ft²). Visitors were able to walk under and even sit on parts of the tube.

The spatial presence of this digitally fabricated tube, on display in the gardens for just one month, makes it seem closer to sculpture than to architecture.

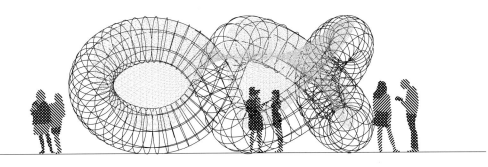

**BORDEN PARK
EDMONTON, CANADA**

**ARCHITECT:
THEVERYMANY**

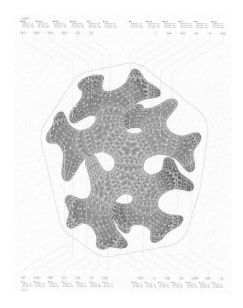

Commissioned by The Edmonton Arts Council this pavilion is described by its architect Marc Fournes as an 'architectural folly', and encompasses self-supporting ultra-thin shells that were assembled from 721 unique digitally fabricated aluminium strips. Although the colours employed were inspired by the natural environment of its location, Borden Park in Edmonton, they were, in the words of the architect, 'pushed toward artificiality' in order to make the structure into a notable and 'iconic destination'. As the architect explains of the unusual structure, 'Vaulted Willow's overall morphology is the result of a reciprocal relationship encompassing experiments in non-linear architectural typology (multiple entries, distributed feet with branching and spiralling legs), structural differentiation (bifurcation of structural download forces, tighter radii of leg profiles for rigidity) and programmatic possibilities for a winding playground (hide and seek).' It took a crew of four to assemble the pavilion – which is 6.1m (20ft) high and 6.7m (22ft) in length and depth – in less than a week. While the design makes transparent the more 'serious' intentions the architect has for it, the structure is also fun and without fear of transgressing architectural stereotypes.

The architects employed some fourteen thousand connectors to join together the 721 aluminim strips that form the pavilion. A total of twenty-four 'legs', or base plates, secure the structure to its concrete base.

MOMA PS1
NEW YORK, USA /
SALAMA BINT HAMDAN FOUNDATION
ABU DHABI, UAE

ARCHITECT:
HWKN

Winner of the 2012 annual Young Architects Program competition, Wendy was installed at MoMA PS1 in the summer of the same year. Made of a nylon mesh fabric treated with a titania nanoparticle spray designed to neutralize airborne pollutants, in the months in which the structure was erected it cleaned the air to the equivalent of taking 260 cars off the road. In addition to producing cool air, mist and jets of water, the spiky structure also projected music out from each of its arms. The design, which envisaged a structure 17 × 17 × 14m (56 × 56 × 46ft) in size, was conceived to form as large a surface area as possible. As Hauke Jungjohann of the engineering consultancy Knippers Helbig explains, 'The magic of Wendy lies in the usage of something simple like a scaffolding system and reinventing its usage so that something new appears that has never been seen before.' Of the name 'Wendy' Matthias Hollwich, founder of HWKN (see also pages 54–55) explains: 'She is a storm that innovates architecture with new ideas of sustainability – and every storm has a name. It breaks down the barrier between architecture and people – it is not just about good-looking buildings – for us it is about personality.' The pavilion was dismantled at the end of the summer and reconstructed in the city of Abu Dhabi during the winter months.

The cutting-edge work as seen in its New York location (here and overleaf).

OBJETS D'ART

**MILAN FURNITURE FAIR
MILAN, ITALY**

**ARCHITECT:
JOHN PAWSON**

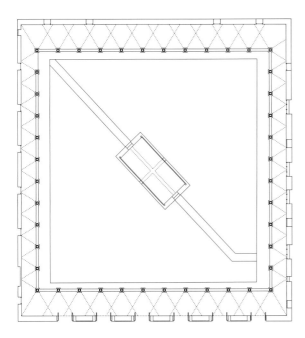

As part of the 2010 Milan Furniture Fair, the Interni Think Tank paired architects and designers with product manufacturers and commissioned them to create installations in various areas of the University of Milan. In this instance, the firm of John Pawson (see also pages 238–39) worked with the stone company Salvatori, employing Lithoverde – a product made from 99 per cent recycled stone (that which is discarded during processing) and 1 per cent binding natural resin – in its design. The structure assumed the form of a simple house with a slightly flattened roof and was positioned in the centre of a courtyard. The architect sliced a gap through the Stone House's mid-section, to allow natural light in and to open up the interior. Thick, protective walls were thus contrasted with the sentiment of the exposure generated by the gap. LED lighting from within made the openings in the house all the more apparent at night. Although the form of the structure does indeed evoke the 'house' that its name implies, the precisely sliced stone implies a kind of permanence that contradicts the ephemeral nature of the installation. Dismounted after the 2010 fair, the Stone House was permanently installed in the park of the Milan Triennale Design Museum.

According to the
architect the project
was inspired by the
architecture of early
English churches
– minimal in design
and made entirely
from stone.

BLUE PAVILION

ROYAL ACADEMY OF ARTS
LONDON, UK

ARCHITECT:
PEZO VON ELLRICHSHAUSEN

Included in the exhibition 'Sensing Spaces: Architecture Reimagined', held at the Royal Academy of Arts in London in 2014, the *Blue Pavilion* was one of seven installations created specifically for the show, and which were installed within the galleries and the courtyard entrance. Kengo Kuma, Alvaro Siza and Eduardo Souto de Moura were among the participants but so too were the slightly less well-known architects Diébédo Francis Kéré and the Chilean duo Mauricio Pezo and Sofia von Ellrichshausen and their firm, Pezo von Ellrichshausen. Built with untreated pine boards, the *Blue Pavilion* was a three-storey structure with a floor area of 152m² (1,636ft²). The architects describe it as 'an elevated small room supported by four massive columns', each of which contained a spiral staircase providing direct access to the upper platform. An enclosed ramp offered yet another route to and from this area. The contrast between the rough pine structure and the surprisingly intimate view offered from the top platform of 'the decorated vaults, the golden angels, the steel beams and the glass skylights of the traditional building' was an interesting effect of the pavilion. So too was the juxtaposition of the 'classical' columns and the coarse materials in which they were composed.

Preliminary sketches
by the architects,
the first (top)
showing from where
the pavilion's
title derives.

In situ in the
galleries of the
Royal Academy;
the enclosed ramp
leading up to the
viewing platform
is located behind
the main structure.

The viewing platform (opposite) and the entry point to one of the spiral stairwells, with the ramp entrance to the left (below).

YOUTURN PAVILION

ARCHITECT:
UNSTUDIO

The 125m² (1,345ft²) Youturn Pavilion was erected by UNStudio (see also pages 60–61) in the context of the 29th São Paulo Biennale in Brazil in 2010. Its CNC-cut plywood rib structure was made up of three repeating modules that were 'rotated' around a central point. Each module was prefabricated and then laminated with thin sheets of plywood that were then plastered, sanded and painted. The structure was erected inside the Cicillo Matarazzo Pavilion, a structure designed by the architect Oscar Niemeyer in 1951, and built in 1954 in Ibirapuera Park as the location for the Biennale, providing some 30,000m² (322,916ft²) of exhibition space for the art fair. In this particular location, the architects explain, Youturn situates 'itself between artwork, installation and architecture'. True to their style, UNStudio employed flowing forms and vivid colours for this striking work.

Views of the installation's interior (opposite, right), and exterior (top) the axis of which is a circular opening at centre (below).

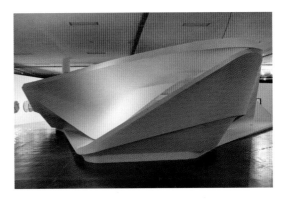

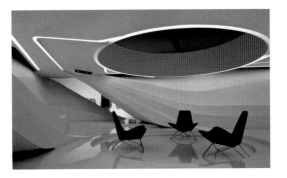

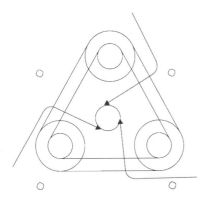

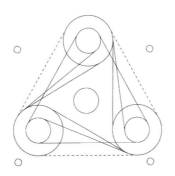

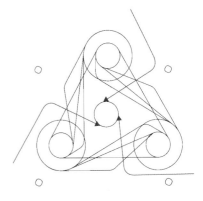

HONG KONG, CHINA

ARCHITECT:
LABORATORY FOR EXPLORATIVE ARCHITECTURE
AND DESIGN (LEAD)

The Golden Moon pavilion was built for Hong Kong's
Mid-Autumn Festival in 2012, and displayed as part
of Lantern Wonderland in Victoria Park for six days.
Constructed in less than two weeks, the structure
employed a combination of digital design technology
and traditional hand craftsmanship. Bamboo was
wrapped around a steel dome and clad – using a
diagonal grid pattern – in 'flames' made of stretchable
fabric that changed colour with the aid of an LED
lighting system. The design was conceived to be quick
to construct and low in cost. The architects explain,
'The Golden Moon revisits the concept of a Chinese
lantern and makes a direct link to the Mid-Autumn
Festival legend of Moon Goddess Chang'e, who can
only meet her husband Houyi on the night of the
Mid-Autumn Festival, when the moon is at its fullest
and most beautiful. To symbolize the passionate love
burning between them, the 6-storey-high, spherical
moon lantern is clad with abstracted flames in fiery
colours and patterns.' Placed on a podium at the
centre of a large pool, the pavilion was large enough
to accommodate 150 visitors, who, on entering the
structure, could experience an exhibition of light and
sound that brought the interior to life. The designers
of this work, LEAD, are a young Hong Kong and
Antwerp-based architectural design and research
practice founded by the Belgian architect Kristof Crolla.

Evoking the appearance of an illuminated moon, Golden Moon was constructed in just eleven days and received some 500,000 visitors during its six-day lifespan.

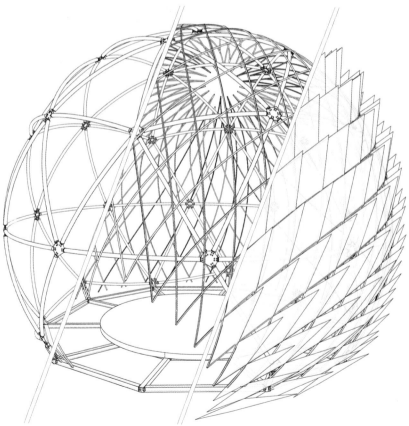

Workers installing the fabric panels on the light steel dome (above), the layout of which was determined by the Fibonacci sequence. A drawing (left) shows the components of the design.

OBJETS D'ART

A drawing of the
interior of the
spherical shell
(right), and the
light display
inside (below).

LEARN

NEW YORK, USA /
BERLIN, GERMANY /
MUMBAI, INDIA

ARCHITECT:
ATELIER BOW-WOW

In 2011 New York's Guggenheim Museum teamed up
with the automobile manufacturer BMW to create this
travelling venue, which was designed by the Japanese
studio Atelier Bow-Wow. This wilfully 'non-iconic'
pavilion was designed with ease of transport in mind
and also had to adapt to each of its different locations.
Its purpose was to offer an educational programme,
entitled 'Confronting Comfort', which included talks,
exhibitions, workshops and screenings, that focused
on the challenges of living in cities. In New York it was
installed in a disused space between two buildings in
the East Village. Covering an area of $217m^2$ ($2,336ft^2$)
it received some 56,000 visitors during its ten-week
residence. Of its identity in this particular location
the architects explain, 'We envisioned a super light
structure that hovers above ground in-between
buildings. The super light structural frame was created
with carbon fibre reinforced plastic, which has the
same strength as steel with one-sixth the weight.
Steel was used in combination for columns to
overcome safety and fire regulations. The space under
the structure is lit uniformly with light filtering through
a polyester roof membrane. The sides of the top half
of the structure are clad with double-layer polyester
mesh, creating a moray effect. At the ground level are
just six columns and a curtain, resulting in architecture
without floors or walls.' In the summer of 2012 the
structure travelled to Berlin, and was constructed at
Prenzlauer Berg in the Pfefferberg complex, a converted
nineteenth-century brewery. After this it travelled
to Mumbai, taking up residence in the city's Byculla
neighbourhood, where it referred to the form of the
mandapa (a traditional outdoor pavilion used for events
and ceremonies). It remained in this location until the
end of January 2013.

Seen in its New York
setting (opposite),
where the Lab created
a programme of events
titled the 'Comfort
Series', and in
Berlin (above),
where it produced
the edition *100
Urban Trends*.

LEARN

The pavilion
in its Mumbai
location, where
its programme
focused on the
theme of public
and private space.

UNDERWOOD PAVILION

MUNCIE, USA

ARCHITECTS:
GERNOT RIETHER / ANDREW WIT

Lead by the directors of Ball State University's Digital Design Build Studio, Gernot Riether and Andrew Wit, the design of the 18m^2 (194ft^2) Underwood Pavilion can best be described as a parametric tensegrity structure. Built with fifty-six modules that form a 'self-shading structural system', it was designed using Rhino-3D, Rhino-Membrane and Kangaroo, with the intention of being easily transportable, 'as a loose low-volume bundle of bars and cables'. Elastane – an 'eco-friendly polymer' that is produced from recycled polyester and used in sportswear such as Lycra – was modified to create the pavilion's 'self-shading envelope'. Working with their students, Riether and Wit brought the modules to site by foot since it could not be accessed in any other way. It took just two days to construct. Intended to draw attention to new cultural events in Muncie, which Riether describes as a city within 'Indiana's Rust Belt', this lightweight design seeks to communicate the advantages of digital design and simplified construction methods using unexpected forms.

The pavilion's
materials – aluminium,
steel and textiles –
refer to the
industries that
were onceprominent
in the region.

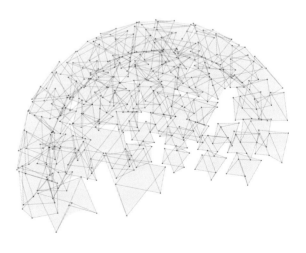

LEARN

The indiviudally
sized tensegrity
modules, grouped
together in a
single form,
appear almost to
be floating, or
about to take
off (below).

LIVING PAVILION

ARCHITECT:
BEHIN HA

FIGMENT is a participatory art event held in various cities throughout the US. In 2010, its organizers teamed up with the New York Architects Committee (ENYA) and the Structural Engineers Association of New York (SEAoNY) to create the City of Dreams competition on Governors Island, the winner of which was a temporary pavilion designed by architects Ann Ha and Behrang Behin. Constructed in the courtyard of Liggett Hall during the summer months, the Living Pavilion was a 'low-tech, zero-impact structure' that stimulated awareness about sustainable architecture. It was built with reclaimed milk crates, which served as a framework on which a 'green wall' could grow. Heavy-duty packaging straps and weather-treated wood were also used in the assembly. Near the vaulted part of the pavilion, the designers placed a 'mat of crates planted with crops that can be harvested and distributed to the community'. The design of the structure and its methods of assembly were conceived so that it would be easy to deconstruct and the elements recycled elsewhere in the city. Ann Ha received a Masters in Architecture from the Harvard Graduate School of Design (GSD) in 2008, where she wrote a thesis entitled 'Reinterpreting Governors Island', a paper focusing on the adaptive reuse of the historic structures on the island, integrating landscape and architecture at different scales. Behrang Behin also graduated from the GSD in 2008 and continued his connection with the institution as an Aga Khan Fellow, studying the 'intersection of technology, architecture, and sustainable urbanism'.

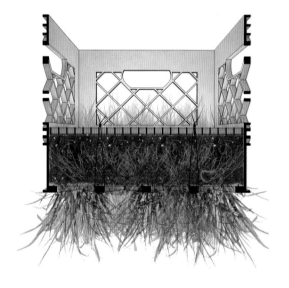

White plastic milk crates, burlap, metal wire and liriope evergreen plants are the main ingredients in this unexpected and small pavilion.

**MATTHAEI BOTANICAL GARDENS
UNIVERSITY OF MICHIGAN, ANN ARBOR, USA**

ARCHITECT:
PLY ARCHITECTURE

Made from more than one hundred aluminium laser-cut cones, the Shadow Pavilion was constructed in the Matthaei Botanical Gardens at the University of Michigan in Ann Arbor in 2009. The intention of the architectural team was to express both the limits of the material and to root the design concept within plant biology (perhaps to compensate for the perceived 'lightness' of the structure in terms of its form and purpose). They explain, 'Organizational schemes for the cones are explored, including the logic behind the concept of phyllotaxis. In botany, phyllotaxis describes a plant's spiral packing arrangement of its elements. The organization of the cones may limit the form, but can strengthen the structure.' The result was 'both a structure and a space made entirely of holes'. The cones were also designed to funnel light and noise into the interior space, offering visitors the opportunity to take in the views and sounds of the surrounding landscape. The pavilion was approximately 4.6 × 9.1m (15 × 30ft) in size. It is one of a number of experimental structures featured in this book – like those designed by ICD / ITKE (pages 118–19) or the Mediated Matter group at MIT (pages 124–25) – and shares with them a reference to the strategies of nature in order to generate unexpected architectural forms. The project was supported by the Research Through Making grant programme run by Ann Arbor's Taubman College.

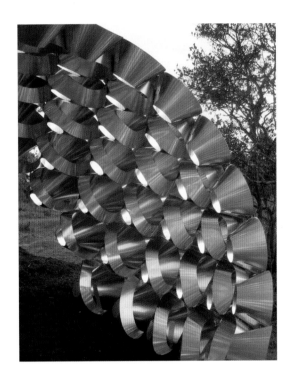

Aluminium cones packed together in a spiral pattern drawing on the forms found in nature give this pavilion an appearance unlike any other built form.

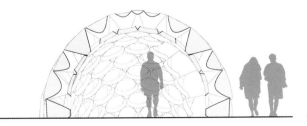

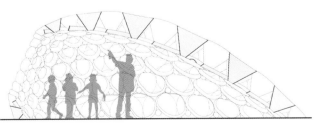

STUTTGART, GERMANY

ARCHITECTS:
INSTITUTE FOR COMPUTATIONAL DESIGN
(ICD) / INSTITUTE OF BUILDING STRUCTURES AND
STRUCTURAL DESIGN (ITKE)

In the summer of 2011, researchers and students from the ICD and the ITKE at the University of Stuttgart designed and built a temporary bionic research pavilion made of birch plywood. They employed innovative computer design and simulation methods together with robotic manufacturing, which enabled the complex structure to be built entirely in thin, 6.5mm (3in) sheets of plywood. The 87m^2 (936ft^2) structure had a volume of 200m^3 (7,062ft^3). The design drew on the structure and form of the skeleton of the sea urchin for inspiration. As the designers explain, 'the interdisciplinary approach based on the integration of architecture, engineering and biology results in an extremely efficient building that offers a unique spatial experience at the same time'. At the heart of this research pavilion is the intention to communicate how the methods employed, based on the forms of nature, could conceivably be put into practice at a larger scale, to develop radically different types of architecture for the future.

The university's robotic fabrication system was used to construct the plates and finger joints of each cell.

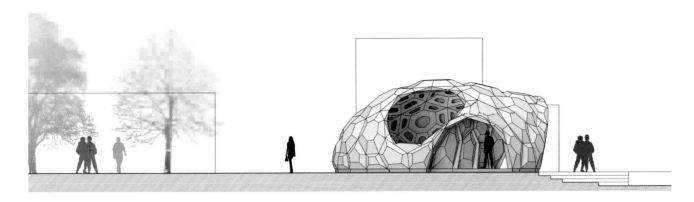

ALLINGE
BORNHOLM, DENMARK

ARCHITECTS:
BENNY JEPSEN / KRISTOFFER TEJLGAARD

In response to a request from BL, Denmark's Public Housing authority, to create a space in which to hold their annual People's Meeting in Bornholm to discuss the future of housing, Kristoffer Tejlgaard and Benny Jepsen (see also pages 130–31) conceived a design in which the optimal construction characteristics of the geodesic dome can be employed in 'deconstructed' form. The result was a structure in which the curved surfaces were closed and the perpendicular ones transparent, a sort of splitting apart in conceptual terms, which was apparent visually. Steel nodes and wood were used in the lattice, which can be disassembled and rebuilt in different configurations. 3D modelling was used to design the skeleton, while the nodes were printed, laser cut and robot welded. The construction timber used was locally harvested Douglas pine. Translucent greenhouse membranes were employed on the spherical surfaces and transparent PVC film was employed for windows. The façade was made with recycled wooden boards. With a floor area of 212m² (2,282ft²), and reaching a maximum height of 8m (24ft), the People's Meeting Dome contains a kitchen, bar, dining area and a stage for debates / performances.

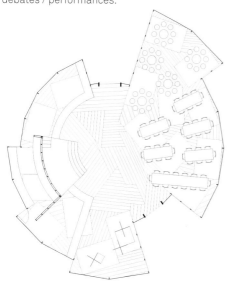

The exterior of
the structure
(below), which brings
to mind an exploded
axonometric drawing
of a geodesic dome.

The architects
alternated closed
and open triangular
sections within
this temporary
structure, to create
a visually dynamic
and unusual space.

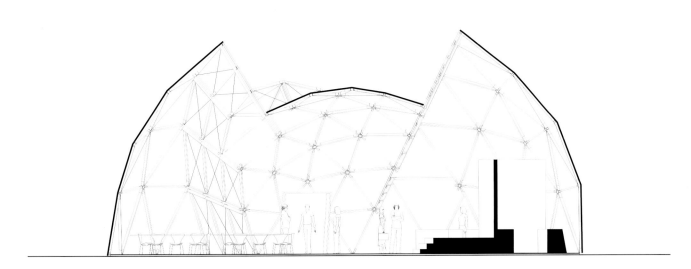

SILK PAVILION

MIT MEDIA LAB
CAMBRIDGE, USA

DESIGNER:
NERI OXMAN

The MIT team programmed a robotic arm to imitate the way silkworms make their cocoons to construct this almost otherworldly structure.

The designer of this pavilion, Neri Oxman, is the Sony Corporation Career Development Professor and Associate Professor of Media Arts and Sciences at the MIT Media Lab. Here she founded and directs the Mediated Matter design research group, which seeks to integrate 'computational form-finding strategies with biologically inspired fabrication'. The group's Silk Pavilion was inspired by the way in which silkworms make their cocoons using a single thread, and was made from twenty-six polygonal panels of silk strands that were applied by a CNC machine. Some 6,500 silkworms were introduced to the project, and were encouraged to 'locally reinforce the gaps across CNC-deposited silk fibres'. With the silkworms gravitating towards darker and denser areas of the construction, light effects were used to 'inform variations across the surface area of the structure'. A sun path diagram was used to determine the location, size and density of openings, and a central oculus placed at top, where it could 'be used as a sun-clock'. Oxman collaborated with Fiorenzo Omenetto (Tufts University) and James Weaver (Wyss Institute, Harvard University) in the making of the structure.

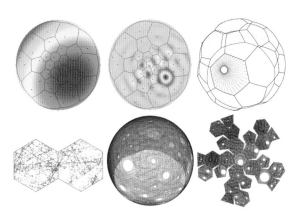

LAVERSTOKE
HAMPSHIRE, UK

ARCHITECT:
HEATHERWICK STUDIO

Founded by Thomas Heatherwick in 1994, the studio that bears his name was, until recently, best known for its product and exhibition design. However, when Heatherwick won the competition to design the UK Pavilion at Expo 2010 in Shanghai it became clear that the designer had far broader ambitions. His first completed commission in the UK involves a site in the village of Laverstoke on the river Test. Originally the location of a corn mill, the land was acquired in 1718 by Henry Portal and developed for the manufacture of paper to produce bank notes. The site was built up over a period of two centuries in what the designer describes as 'an uncoordinated accumulation of over forty buildings'. The complex included a number of Grade II listed buildings, which had been abandoned and left derelict for a number of years before being acquired by Bacardi as a site for the manufacture of Bombay Sapphire, its own brand of gin. The company called on Heatherwick to refurbish the site, which involved creating a distillery and a visitor's centre. Heatherwick's scheme envisioned a central courtyard as a gathering point and focus for the site. The visitor's centre was an unconventional pavilion within this space and was formed of two intertwining botanical glasshouses, one with a tropical climate and the other Mediterranean. The asymmetrical structures are made from 893 individually crafted pieces of glass supported by bronze-finished stainless steel frames. Within each one the ten plant species that give Bombay Sapphire gin its particular taste are cultivated, enabling visitors to experience first-hand the distillery process. The distillery received an 'outstanding' BREEAM rating for its design, making it not only the first distillery but the first refurbishment project to have been awarded this distinction.

The flowing, organic
lines of the
greenhouse structure
intersect with one
of the historical
buildings (left).
A section drawing
(below) shows the
airflow throughout
the complex.

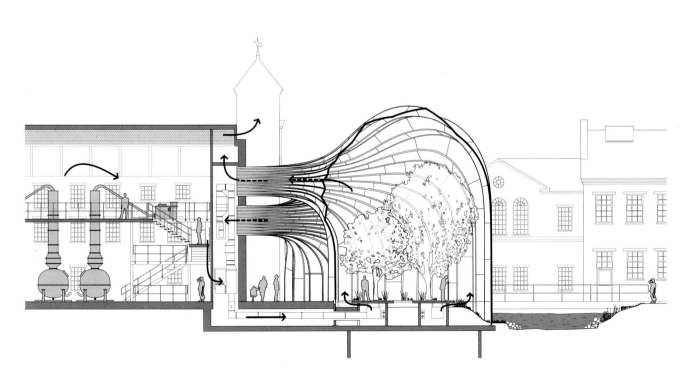

HEATHERWICK STUDIO

COPENHAGEN, DENMARK

ARCHITECTS:
BENNY JEPSEN / KRISTOFFER TEJLGAARD

Located in the harbour area of Copenhagen at Krøyers Square, the Dome of Visions is a temporary structure that was constructed to house a variety of events, including debates about the future of sustainable housing, performances and concerts. Under a 346m² (3,724ft²) geodesic dome design, the architects erected a 71m² (764ft²) two-storey wooden 'house' and a further 274m² (2,950ft²) of terraces and gardens. They collaborated with the Danish firm NCC for this project, which, after it had served its purpose in Copenhagen, was transported to Aarhus. The architects (see also pages 120–23) used CNC-cut polycarbonate sheeting, which was overlapped in order to protect the structure from both wind and rain. The garden was planted with eucalyptus trees, an olive tree, grape vines, peach trees, apple trees and flowers. In its prominent harbour location, the Dome of Visions represents a relatively light expression of some very contemporary ideas in architecture, combined with Buckminster Fuller's already venerable geodesic dome. Ecologically responsible and modern, the Dome of Visions demonstrates how temporary pavilions can encourage thought and debate.

The façade of this geodesic dome was covered in a total of 256 transparent plates, to allow light in and retain an ambient internal climate.

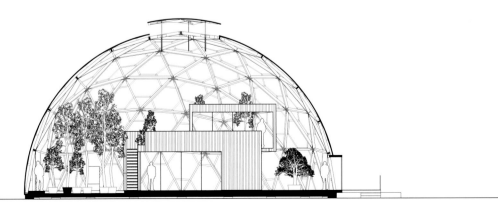

WHITNEY STUDIO

WHITNEY MUSEUM OF AMERICAN ART
NEW YORK, USA

ARCHITECT:
LOT-EK

Made from six shipping containers stacked on two levels, magnesium oxide (MGO) boards and steel, this 60m² (646ft²) pavilion was placed at the south end of the Whitney Museum's external 'moat' and served as temporary studio space. Commissioned by the museum's education department, the structure functioned as an area in which art workshops, special exhibitions and small lectures could be held. A white, double-height area for the display of works of art formed the main interior while a triangular mezzanine was used for storage. The containers were cut diagonally along two sides and the roof of the volume to allow in natural light and let passers-by view the studio's activities. Founded by Ada Tolla and Giuseppe Lignano, both of Italian origin, LOT-EK has been based in New York and Naples since 1995. LOT-EK has done a great deal of work in the area of temporary pavilions for such clients as Uniqlo, Puma (pages 150–51) and the Van Alen Institute.

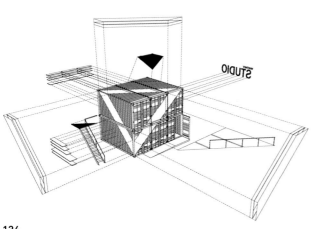

Each of the six
containers was
modified and painted
off-site before being
carefully craned
into position in the
sculpture court of
the Marcel Brauer-
designed building.

LWL MUSEUM FOR ART AND
CULTURAL HISTORY
MÜNSTER, GERMANY

ARCHITECT:
MODULORBEAT

This temporary pavilion was created for the exhibition
'Golden Glory: Medieval Treasury Art in Westphalia',
held at the LWL Museum for Art and Cultural History
on the Domplatz in Münster in 2012. Renovation work
on the museum and the desire of the exhibition curators
to show how some of the work exhibited was made
inspired the idea of adding a small (95m^2/1,023ft^2)
pavilion on the Domplatz itself, for staging workshops
demonstrating artisanal goldwork techniques. The
Münster-based architects modulorbeat, headed by
Marc Günnewig and Jan Kampshoff, were commissioned
to design the building. They had already created
a portable, temporary construction in 2007 for the
'Skulptur Projekte Münster' that was notable because
of its golden colour. The Golden Workshop was designed
and built in collaboration with students from the
Münster School of Architecture. The cross-shaped
structure was made essentially in plywood and covered
with vertical copper and aluminium alloy metal panels,
with four wings opening onto the central workshop.
Made from TECU® Gold, the panels had a luminous
quality when exposed to sunlight. Full-height glazed
windows at the end of each wing permitted views in and
out. The total cost of the building was approximately
£115,540 (€160,000).

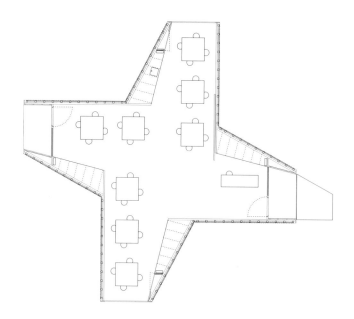

The four-winged
structure was planned
and constructed in
just six weeks. At
the end of each wing
is a large glass
window, allowing
views into and out
from the workshop.

LIVERPOOL BIENNIAL
LIVERPOOL, UK

ARCHITECT / ARTIST:
DAVID ADJAYE / DOUG AITKEN

A temporary pavilion made from timber, acoustic foam, corrugated polycarbonate and bitumen board, The Source was the result of a collaboration between the London-based architect David Adjaye and the American artist Doug Aitken, and erected for the 2013 Tate Liverpool Biennial. Aitken is renowned for his innovative installations and Adjaye for his work with cultural organizations the world over, including his Bernie Grant Arts Centre in London and the Museum of Contemporary Art in Denver in the US, both 2007. They first joined forces in 2005 to work on *Broken Screen: 26 Conversations with Doug Aitken*, a publication that featured interviews with a variety of cultural figures, ranging from Werner Herzog to Rem Koolhaas.

At 160m² (1,722ft²), The Source was erected on Albert Dock, just next to Tate Liverpool. Inside, films of Aitken's conversations with cultural figures, including the artists James Turrell and Philippe Pareno, the musician Jack White, the architect Jacques Herzog, and David Adjaye himself, were projected. Aitken and Adjaye explain the concept of the project: 'The temporary structure is a deliberate device to separate the work from the traditional gallery space and to create a new cultural territory. The collage of imagery and interviews radiates within a diorama – a cylindrical chamber – inside which six projections are simultaneously displayed in six little rooms. As visitors cross the bridge over to Tate Liverpool, the structure is almost unavoidable. Although the projections are on the inside, they have a ghost image on the exterior – especially at night to attract people inside.'

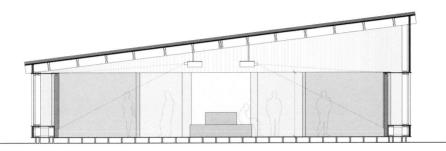

The interior of the pavilion had several viewing areas, as seen in a section drawing (left). Aitken's films were also visible from the exterior (below).

MILAN TRIENNALE
MILAN, ITALY

ARCHITECT:
SHIGERU BAN

Built to showcase a new range of furniture by the Finnish furniture company Artek at the Milan Triennale in 2007, this temporary pavilion was made of UPM ProFi, a wood-plastic composite. UPM, also a Finnish company, was involved at the request of the client, and Shigeru Ban (see also pages 232–34) employed the material within a truss structure. Made of 70 per cent paper and 30 per cent plastic, ProFi can be extruded in the shape of boards or other elements used in the construction of buildings. Capable of being worked with much like wood, the substance is lightweight and doesn't require supplementary coating for outdoor use. Here, even the beams and cross-members are made of ProFi and held together with steel plates. Erected in April 2007, and conceived as a mobile venue for the display of Artek's products that would travel to other locations after the Milan Triennale, the pavilion was 5.88m (19ft) high, 40m (131ft) long and 185m² (1,991ft²). Shaped somewhat like a house, its roof had transparent panelling at the centre to allow sunlight into the exhibition area. Ban is noted for his use of paper as a structural element in his designs. In this instance, using an innovative paper-based product, he created a simple, economical and ecologically responsible space in which the work of the Finnish company might be promoted and the influence of its founder, Alvar Aalto, on Ban's own practice acknowledged.

The structure of the pavilion is simple and repetitive (right, opposite). Industrial and agricultural buildings inform the design, built for the purpose of showcasing Artek's new bamboo range (above).

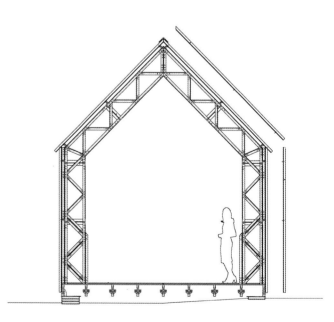

LONDON, UK

ARCHITECT:
SERIE ARCHITECTS

Drawing on the Victorian bandstand as an unexpected source of inspiration for their pavilion, Serie Architects note, 'The British have a particular fondness for the Victorian bandstand. Comprised of a lightweight roof supported on exposed slender columns the idea of the bandstand is to get close to nature by stripping back the architecture to a minimum. There is no role for exotic form and shape-making: the architecture's beauty comes not from itself but rather from its open attitude to its natural surroundings.' Located on the Waterworks river in the Olympic Park, the BMW Group Pavilion was conceived to include a light plinth covered, in parts, with water drawn from the neighbouring river, which was then filtered and sterilized, so that the structure became a kind of 'liquid podium'. The architects also refer to the carbon fibre bodywork of BMW's electric and hybrid cars in the roof of the structure, which is realized as a series of timber 'shells'. The areas of display were imagined as a series of nine grouped pavilions with a total area of approximately 1,600m^2 (17,222ft^2) that could be separated and used elsewhere after the events of 2012.

The floating structure
was moored next to
the ArcelorMittal
Orbit, designed by
Anish Kapoor and
Cecil Balmond
(below). An exploded
axonometric drawing
(left) shows the
arrangement of the
roof canopies.

MOBILE ART PAVILION FOR CHANEL

HONG KONG, CHINA /
TOKYO, JAPAN /
NEW YORK, USA /
PARIS, FRANCE

ARCHITECT:
ZAHA HADID ARCHITECTS

Inspired by the design of the celebrated 2.55 quilted handbag made famous by Coco Chanel in 1955, the Mobile Art Pavilion was commissioned by Karl Lagerfeld in 2007, and designed by Zaha Hadid Architects (see also pages 158–59). 'She is the first architect to find a way to part with the all-dominating post-Bauhaus aesthetic,' Lagerfeld explained at the launch of the Mobile Art Pavilion at the 2007 Venice Biennale. 'The value of her is similar to that of great poetry. The potential of her imagination is enormous.' The arch-shaped structure included a 65m^2 (700ft^2) central courtyard and a partially glazed, adjustable ceiling, and has been described as a 'new artificial landscape for art installations'. At 6m (20ft) high, 29m (95ft) long and 45m (148ft) wide, and with a total floor area of 700m^2 (7,537ft^2), it was designed for easy disassembly and shipment. Of the project Hadid explains, 'The complexity and technological advances in in digital imaging software and construction techniques have made the architecture of the Mobile Art Pavilion possible. It is an architectural language of fluidity and nature, driven by new digital design and manufacturing processes, which have enabled us to create the Pavilion's totally organic forms – instead of the serial order of repetition that marks the architecture of the industrial twentieth century.' First constructed in Hong Kong in March 2008, the structure travelled to New York, where it was installed at Rumsey Playfield in Central Park from 20 October to 9 November the same year. There were plans for it to tour to London, Moscow and Paris, however this part of the schedule was cancelled by Chanel. In early 2011, the company donated the pavilion to the Institut du monde Arabe in Paris, where it was built on the entrance parvis, and finally dismantled in April 2014.

The pavilion in New York (opposite), and the interior (above).

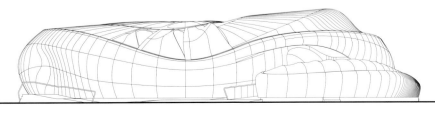

YEOSU EXPO HYUNDAI MOTOR GROUP PAVILION

YEOSU, SOUTH KOREA

**ARCHITECT:
UNSANGDONG ARCHITECTS**

Built on a site measuring 1,960m² (21,098ft²) and with a total floor area of 2,334m² (25,122ft²) this steel-frame pavilion is made up of 'contrasting three-dimensional frames'. The image of the 'blue ocean' was a source of inspiration for the designers, in response to which they have created a number of moving elements, including large screens that have been installed both in front of and behind the building to project a combination of bright and colourful 'free flowing images' that draw attention to the structure. The visual displays can be accessed from either end of the pavilion through corridors that run along its perimeter. An interactive wall, dubbed the 'Hyper Matrix', is located at the building's centre. The intention of the architects was to design a structure that reflected the commitment of the car manufacturer, Hyundai, to the 'relationship between the natural environment and digital technology', as well as the 'entrepreneurial spirit of the brand through its energetic form'. Essentially, the themes of the pavilion are 'motion' and 'change'. The undulating forms of the façade are meant to symbolize the 'waves' of technology and transport advancing toward the future, or the idea that the brand is continuously progressive.

The pavilion in situ (opposite) and in an elevation drawing of the main façade (opposite). Visitors could enter into the structure and walk behind the illuminated screens (above).

**ALICANTE, SPAIN /
BOSTON, USA**

**ARCHITECT:
LOT-EK**

PUMACity's simple
design, encompassing
only shipping
containers, was
transported to and
reconstucted in two
further locations
after Alicante:
Boston and Stockholm.

LOT-EK (see also pages 134–35) used shipping containers as the primary material in the design of this moveable retail and event building. Twenty-four 12m (39ft) containers were stacked on three levels with a cantilevered design that allowed for outdoor terraces, and to give the impression of sliding volumes that could be adapted to each new location. The exterior and interior walls were bright red and the white Puma logo featured on the outside. The pavilion included offices, storage space, a bar and an event area. The impetus behind this architectural gesture was to create a structure that could follow a Puma-sponsored sailboat during the 2008 Volvo Ocean Race. As the architects explain, 'PUMACity is a truly experimental building that takes full advantage of the global shipping network already in place. At 11,000 square feet of space, it will be the first container building of its scale to be truly mobile, designed to respond to all of the architectural challenges of a building of its kind, including international building codes, dramatic climate changes and ease of assembly and operations.' The pavilion was first constructed in Alicante in Spain, in time for the opening of the race on 11 October 2008.

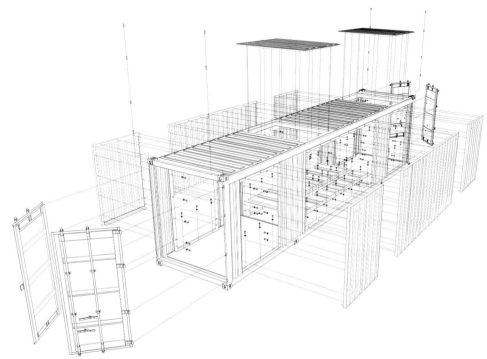

LOT-EK

SHANGHAI, CHINA

ARCHITECT:
ATELIER FCJZ

This unexpected and colourful pavilion was built with a polycarbonate plastic façade, which could be broken down and recycled after use, and relied on solar power and the collection of rainwater for much of its energy. Built for Expo 2010 Shanghai, it was on site from 1 May to 31 October. In keeping with the Expo's ambitions, the structure was both innovative and environmentally responsible in its design. Beyond these criteria, FCJZ (see also pages 200–03) sought to make the structure flexible in its appearance and potential use. As the architects explain: 'The interior spaces of the Shanghai Corporate Pavilion, which are shaped as a series of free, flowing forms, will be no longer enclosed by walls of the static kind but a dense, cubic volume of infrastructural network, including LED lights and a mist-making system, which are capable of changing the appearance of the building from one moment to another as programmed through a computer.' A 1,600m^2 (17,222ft^2) heat-collecting solar tube was placed on the roof of the building, and the rainwater collection system was used to produce a mist, which lowers the internal temperature to provide a comfortable climate within the pavilion, itself comprising a floor area of nearly 5,000m^2 (53,820ft^2). Yung Ho Chang and his wife Lijia Lu established the Beijing firm FCJZ in 1993.

In their design the architects hoped 'to visually convey the…dream of a brighter future, through sophisticated technologies'.

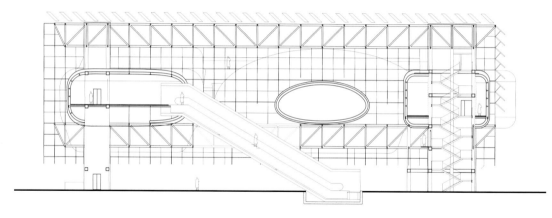

HEEMSKERK, THE NETHERLANDS

ARCHITECT:
ANNE HOLTROP

Born in The Netherlands in 1977, Anne Holtrop studied at the Academy of Architecture in Amsterdam between 1999 and 2005. His work, however, seems as closely related to art as it is to architecture, and he claims that his initial drawings for the Temporary Museum (Lake) were 'made by chance': 'Chance struck me as a way of making work that does not make reference to anything specific. But the mind of the viewer, like my mind, wishes to see things in them, like in a Rorschach inkblot. Jumping between different visions the mind projects its own ideas on it. Each construction, each gesture is a new reality. So is the use of one of these drawings to make the temporary museum.' The 50m² (538ft²) structure was erected in a nature reserve near Amsterdam and took six weeks to build. Made from untreated laminated poplar it was a single-level space that sought to make the distinction between the inside and outside 'ambiguous'. This apparent reference to Japanese tradition is supported by a design in which there is no point at which the whole exterior (or interior) of the pavilion could be viewed in its entirety. The result, as Holtrop puts it, was that 'the experience of the building is always relational, and not the experience of an absolute whole'. The pavilion functioned as a 'museum' for the work of four artists – Renie Spoelstra, Eva-Fiore Kovacovsky, Driessens & Verstappen and Sjoerd Buisman – and was dismantled after just six weeks.

The unexpected
amorphous lake-shaped
pavilion is visible
in its plan (right),
but is difficult to
perceive at ground
level (above, opposite).

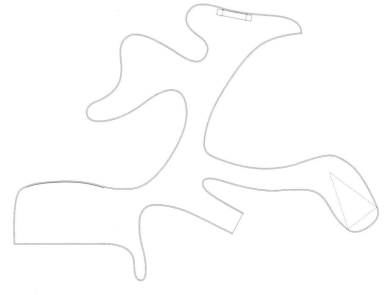

ANNE HOLTROP

**MILLENNIUM PARK
CHICAGO, USA**

**ARCHITECT:
ZAHA HADID ARCHITECTS**

Zaha Hadid's (see also pages 146–47) Burnham
Pavilion, along with another temporary structure,
designed by Ben van Berkel (UNStudio; pages 60–61),
was located in Millennium Park in Chicago. The purpose
of this event was to celebrate the centenary of the
Plan of Chicago, co-authored by the architects/urban
planners Daniel Burnham and Edward Bennett in 1909.
The 120m^2 (1,290ft^2) Burnham Pavilion was designed
by Hadid to house a multimedia work by Thomas D. Gray
(The Gray Circle), which conceived of a 'moving-image
installation of Chicago past, present and future'. Made
from seven thousand pieces of individually bent
aluminium, the structure was covered by a fabric
membrane both inside and out. The pavilion contained
'hidden traces of Burnham's organizational structure'
in the form of the diagonal lines across the roof. Of
the concept Hadid explains, 'The presence of the new
structure triggers the visitor's intellectual curiosity
whilst an intensification of public life around and within
the pavilion supports the idea of public discourse.'

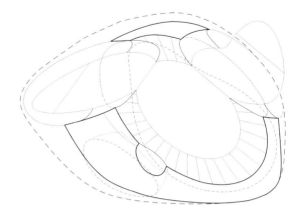

Hadid's design
was conceived
to maximize the
recycling and re-use
of the pavilion's
materials after
its dismantlement.

VIDEBÆK, DENMARK

ARCHITECT:
HENNING LARSEN

Located in Videbæk Park in the Jutland peninsula in western Denmark, Henning Larsen's Art Pavilion has been compared by the architect to a traditional Japanese tea house in its appearance and function. Intended to be flexible in terms of its use, the pavilion is essentially one large space, which can be altered by the installation of lightweight walls for temporary exhibitions. It also includes a café, which faces onto the lake. An overhead skylight encourages natural light into the 400m^2 (4,306ft^2) structure, which itself is essentially made up of two horizontal planes that are divided by a glass façade and a 'varied system of inclined façade parts'. According to the architects, 'The musical, intersecting façade is inspired by the surrounding landscape, the rushes of the lake and branches of the trees. The geometry can also be considered a play with Videbæk's landmark, the V.'

The material Troldtekt was chosen as the material for the ceiling due to its acoustic properties, and was used both inside and out.

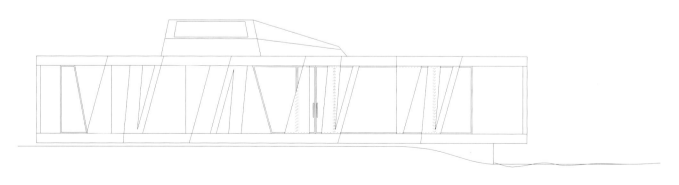

NEW YORK, USA

ARCHITECT:
SO-IL

The Storefront for Art and Architecture is a non-profit organization that was founded in 1982 by Kyontg Park to promote innovation in the fields of art, architecture and design. In 2015 it held the exhibition 'Blueprint' – curated by the architects Florian Idenburg and Jing Liu of SO-IL, and the Dutch artist Sebastiaan Bremer – which invited artists and architects to 'reflect on the theme of origination through the medium of the blueprint'. The show, the title of which referred to an exhibition of the same name organized by Bremer and Pieter Woudt in 1998, comprised fifty blueprints, dating from 1961 to 2013. Working with the existing structure, built in 1993 to the designs of the architect Steven Holl and the artist Vito Acconci, the 'Blueprint' installation involved the transformation of the pivoting façade by shrink-wrapping it into 'one continuous and undulating surface'. As Idenburg and Liu explain, 'Rather than conserve, this shrink-wrap reinvigorates the existing Holl-Acconci installation and reveals the activities happening behind its permeable skin.'

The undulating façade of the building, the structure of which can be seen in an exploded axonometric drawing (opposite) and at night, when the space is illuminated (overleaf), was essentially 'vacuum-packed' by the external white 'skin'.

EXHIBIT

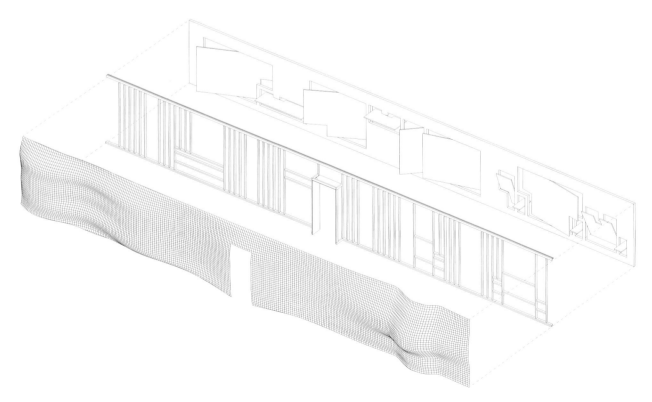

CHINA PAVILION

EXPO MILANO
MILAN, ITALY

ARCHITECT:
STUDIO LINK-ARC / TSINGHUA UNIVERSITY

Rather than creating a 'cultural pavilion as an object in a plaza', the architects sought to define their work in Milan as a 'field of spaces'. The most visible element of the design is an undulating roof layered with bamboo shingles, the intention of which is to visually unite the profiles of the landscape to the south and the city to the north of the site. A 'raised-beam' system in wood traditionally used in Chinese buildings allowed for generous space below. Wheat was planted around the structure in reference to the agrarian history of China. An LED multimedia presentation is located at centre, around which a platform was installed to offer visitors views of the Expo and the surrounding areas. The landscape and interior design were carried out by Tsinghua University, as were the lighting and the visual identity of the pavilion.

The multimedia installation contained within this freeform timber structure contained some twenty-two thousand LED 'stalks'.

EXHIBIT

The striking,
undulating form
of the pavilion
when illuminated.

CESSNOCK, AUSTRALIA

ARCHITECT:
PETER STUTCHBURY

This building, essentially comprised of a folded, curving roof, won the Colorbond Award for Steel Architecture at Australia's 2011 National Architecture Awards.

Although aeroplane hangars generally have a single function, in this instance the structure also operates as a gallery and museum. Taking advantage of the space required for the movement of the aircraft, the building 'is essentially utilitarian, yet offers visitors a memorable "aeronautical" experience'. The design refers to the vaulted 'blister' hangars of the Second World War that were intended to be invisible from the air, but also has the visual appearance of the profile of an aeroplane wing. With four main trusses the building is covered with 15m (49ft) spans of Aramax roof sheeting. The curved vault truss was designed to support the 12m (39ft) cantilever of the awning and to allow for a 30m (98ft) sliding door. The structural system was studied to reduce the usage of steel by as much as 30 per cent. A suspended walkway measuring 45m (148ft) in length allows visitors to observe the planes and connects the administrative 'pods' situated to the east and west of the building. Simply put, as the architect explains: 'The hangar is a well-planned and serviced volume, which is economical and environmentally responsible, while creating a theatrical public window into aviation history.' Cessnock Aerodrome, where the Hangar is located, is an hour north of Sydney, in the Hunter Valley, an area noted for its wine production. The Hangar is home to Air Action, an aviation museum with a collection of vintage fighter planes.

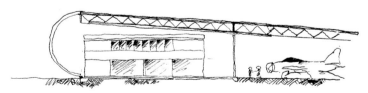

LOOK /

LISTEN

JELLYFISH THEATRE

LONDON, UK

ARCHITECTS:
MARTIN KALTWASSER / FOLKE KÖEBBERLING

The entrances to the 'lounge' area and auditorium. The recuperation of used pallets, panels and planks gives the ecologically responsible structure an improvised appearance.

Built in a south London playground, this temporary theatre was made in large part from scrapped theatre sets, reclaimed timber, market pallets and old kitchen units, the result being that one *Guardian* critic heralded it as a milestone in the rise of 'junkitecture'. Commissioned in 2010 by the theatre company The Red Room for the London Festival of Architecture's Oikos Project, the structure was built largely by a group of volunteers. About the project, *Financial Times* critic Sarah Hemming noted: 'It looks fantastic – rather graceful in its idiosyncratic way. It sits in a school playground not far from London Bridge like a resting spaceship from a particularly right-on planet. It is a low structure, clad in a jaunty patchwork of wooden panels, extended fore and aft by pallets and planks that give it the rough shape of a boat (a junk, perhaps) and festooned with decorated water bottles.' Kaltwasser's and Köebberling's backgrounds in art can certainly be felt in this project, with its combination of event-driven installation, performance and public art.

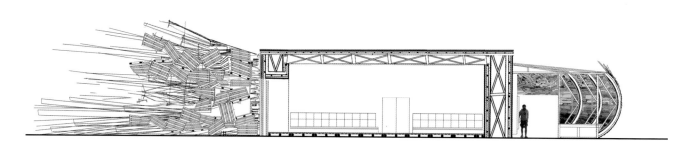

LOOK / LISTEN

The back of the
structure and the free-
form accumulations of
wood on the exterior
house theatre dressing
rooms (left). A detail
of the lounge (above).

NO99 STRAW THEATRE

SKOONE BASTION
TALLINN, ESTONIA

ARCHITECT:
SALTO AB

Created in the year Tallinn was designated European Capital of Culture, this temporary 440m² (4,736ft²) theatre was built in the centre of the city, atop the baroque fortification of Skoone bastion. Aside from being the site for performances, the structure was also intended to draw attention to the bastion itself, which had been closed for twenty years, since the end of Soviet rule. Located on the site of a former theatre, the new design incorporated a staircase from the earlier structure. This element forms the stepped access, which is the only part of the plan that deviates from and extends the simple rectangular footprint. The building itself was made of exposed bales of hay, spray-painted black and reinforced with trusses, the result being that the structure had no need for insulation, something to which the architects refer to emphasize its sustainability. On site only for the summer of 2011, the NO99 Straw Theatre was surrounded by external features such as a giant chessboard, tennis tables, swings and a baking oven, providing the area 'with a non-commercial and pleasantly low-key feel'.

The Tallinn-based
architects won the
Estonian Culture
Endowment Prize
in Architecture
in 2012 for their
sustainable design.

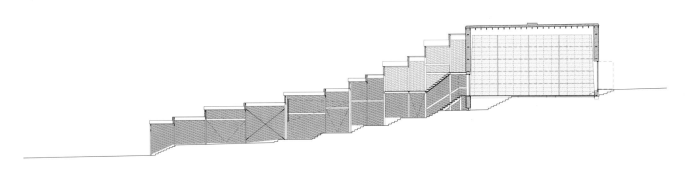

MARGARET WHITLAM PAVILION

NATIONAL ARBORETUM
CANBERRA, AUSTRALIA

ARCHITECT:
TONKIN ZULAIKHA GREER

The axis of the
building is aligned
with the Capital
Hill node from the
architect Walter
Burley Griffin's
Canberra plan.

In 2004, Tonkin Zulaikha Greer, in association with the landscape architects Taylor Cullity Lethlean, won a competition to design a pavilion for Canberra's National Arboretum, a 290-hectare (716-acre) site located north of the city's Lake Burley Griffin. The Margaret Whitlam Pavilion, completed in 2013, includes a central internal space that can be used for social events and performances, and which can accommodate up to one hundred people. To the east, the pavilion opens onto an outdoor terrace and offers views of the city and nearby mountains, with smaller terraces to the north and south, all with glass doors that can be fully opened, offering scenes of the surrounding landscape. Its steel beam structure employs insulating composite panels and it is clad on the exterior in zinc. Water recycling and other 'low-energy' services ensure the sustainability of the building. The dramatic forward-angled roof makes the structure a striking addition to the area, which can be seen from the main entry to the arboretum.

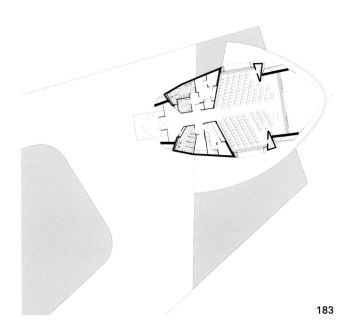

NORWEGIAN WILD REINDEER
CENTRE PAVILION

HJERKINN
DOVREFJELL NATIONAL PARK, NORWAY

ARCHITECT:
SNØHETTA

Aside from being a well-known architectural practice based in Oslo, who were responsible for the design of this pavilion (see also pages 66–67), Snøhetta is also the name of a mountain – the largest in a range at Dovrefjell National Park in Norway – around which a good deal of local mythology is centred. In 2011 the architects were commissioned by the park's Wild Reindeer Foundation to create a pavilion that would serve as an educational centre and offer spectacular views of the landscape and wildlife, including the reindeer that live there. On the outside a strict rectangular volume, the pavilion has a surprising 'rippled' pine interior. This organic, curved internal space was created using 3D digital modelling and CNC milling, and manufactured by shipbuilders. The wooden structures were joined together using only pegs in the same material, and their surfaces preserved in oil. The exterior walls are coated in a protective layer of pine tar. The architects explain, 'In essence the building is about shelter. It allows for groups of people to gather whilst looking at the magnificent mountain scenery or wait for a glimpse of wild reindeer herds or Musk oxen. The cave-like wooden core with its integrated benches is a soft interpretation of the intimacy generated between people and landscape where one is depending on the other.'

The 90m² (969ft²) pavilion was built at an altitude of 1,220m (4,000ft) at a cost of around £385,180 (€530,000).

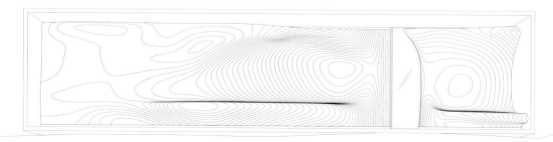

LOOK / LISTEN

As seen from the
exterior, the pavilion
conveys geometric
simplicity in contrast
to its rough, natural
environment.

MARSEILLE VIEUX PORT
PAVILION

MARSEILLE, FRANCE

ARCHITECT:
FOSTER + PARTNERS

In 2013 Foster + Partners were commissioned to produce a masterplan for the Vieux Port area of Marseille, a UNESCO World Heritage site. The 100,000m² (1,076,391ft²) scheme, carried out at the request of MPM (Marseille Provence Metropole), sought to 'reclaim the quaysides as a civic space, creating new, informal venues for performances and events and removing traffic to create a safe, semi-pedestrianized public realm'. The project was carried out in the same year the city was awarded the status of European Capital of Culture. The landscape design, which included a new pale granite surface for the area, was produced in partnership with landscape architect Michel Desvigne. Located at the eastern side of the harbour, on the Quai des Belges, Foster + Partners conceived of the Vieux Port pavilion as a 'dramatic blade' of reflective stainless steel, one that would offer shelter to passers-by and form a space in which events could take place. Measuring 46 × 22m (151 × 72ft), and tapering toward its edges, the mirrored canopy has slender pillars as supports. Literally reflecting its location, and being unobtrusive in form, the pavilion sensitively blends into its environment without imposing itself as a grand architectural gesture.

The architects'
approach, they explain,
was 'to work with the
climate, to create
shade, but at the same
time to respect the
space of the harbour'.

MUNICH, GERMANY

ARCHITECT:
COOP HIMMELB(L)AU

With such significant works as the Musée des Confluences in Lyon, in France, completed in 2014, the Vienna-based firm Coop Himmelb(l)au remains an active force in contemporary architecture, long after its inclusion in the seminal 1988 exhibition 'Deconstructivist Architecture' at the Museum of Modern Art in New York. In 2010, they designed the 430m^2 (4,628ft^2) Pavilion 21 for the Bavarian State Opera in Munich, with the purpose of being a temporary, mobile performance space that could be used during the annual Opera Festival. The acoustics were overseen by the engineering firm Arup. Installed in the city's Marstallplatz it was large enough to house an audience of three hundred. The architects explain of their concept, 'The design approach studies the impact of physical influences on our hearing perception and how to apply soundscape effects to alter our sensation through transforming and adopting building volumes and their material specifications.' The architects sought literally to 'materialize music into architecture' by using the songs of Jimi Hendrix amongst others to generate the exterior form of the pavilion. The aluminium structure was built at a cost of around £1,520,000 (€2.1 million) and was sponsored by BMW/MINI.

```
The spiky structure
was fitted out with
a combination of
perforating (absorbent)
and smooth (reflective)
panels in order to
meet acoustic
requirements.
```

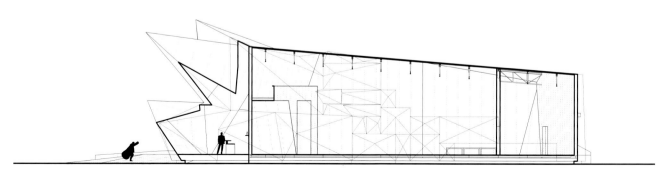

The pavilion was
designed to be easy
to construct and
deconstruct, with the
intention of it being
assembled in various
locations after its
realization in Munich.

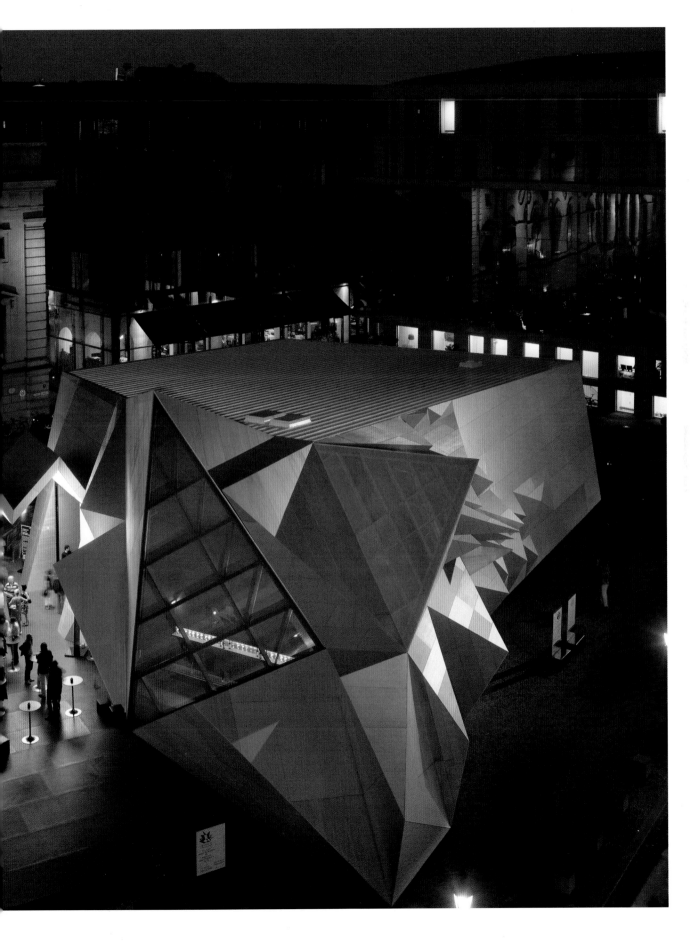

VALENCIA
SANTA CLARITA, USA

ARCHITECT:
HPLUSF ARCHITECTS

In 1985 Los Angeles architects Craig Hodgetts and Hsin-Ming Fung joined forces to found the firm Hodgetts + Fung. Now called HplusF Architects, the studio has produced a number of venues for the performing arts. In 2010 they were invited by the California Institute of Arts (CalArts) to design a multipurpose performance space that could seat 120 spectators and which would function both as an indoor recital hall and classroom and as an open-air orchestra shell. To achieve this, the architects designed one wall entirely in glass that could be opened in the form of a folding awning, and the sound projected out towards the audience. The 228m^2 (2,453ft^2) structure has a monocoque roof that was designed for acoustic clarity. The architects state, 'This volume is also defined by a single thin, folded plane, which derives its strength from a pure geometric configuration which is not only structurally efficient but provides a dramatic contrast to the massive rectilinearity of the surrounding buildings.' Forming a continuous curve, the roof and the back wall are clad in copper shingles. The concept of the pavilion and its name are something of a homage to the composer Morton Feldman (1926–1987), who said that the 'wild beast lives in the jungle and not in the zoo'. He also expressed his interest in 'elegant but minimal musical strategies', something which the architects have sensitively articulated in this design.

The design incorporated movable surfaces, which could be rotated, pivoted and opened to accommodate a wide range of performance requirements.

I AM
INTERESTED
IN HOW
THE WILD BEAST
LIVES IN
THE JUNGLE,
NOT IN
THE ZOO.

MORTON FELDMAN

A drawing (opposite) of the access ramp shows the back and spine of a 'wild beast', a form not so apparent at ground level (below). The cantilevered roof (left), which is clad in copper-coloured shingles.

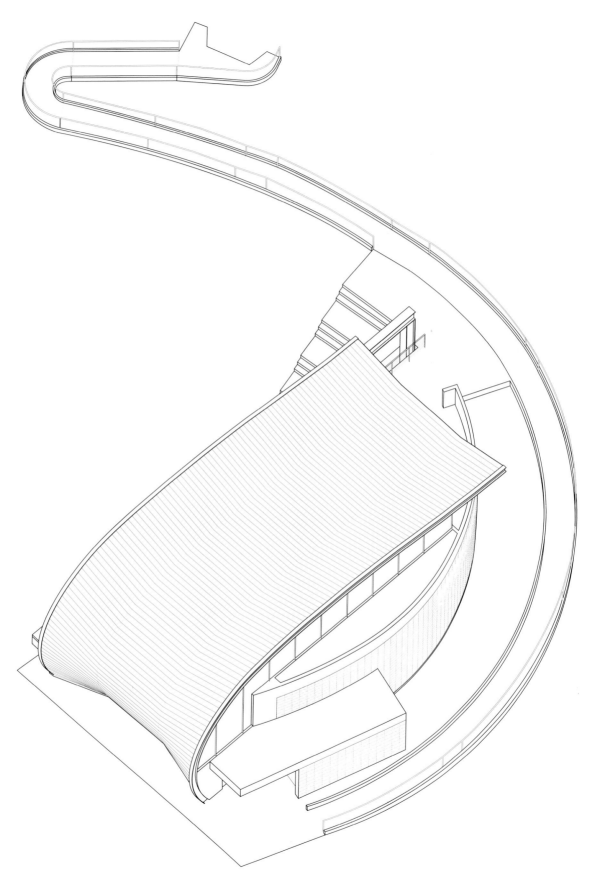

LIVE /

WORK /

VERTICAL GLASS HOUSE

SHANGHAI, CHINA

ARCHITECT:
ATELIER FCJZ

Designed by FCJZ (see also pages 152–55) founder
Yung Ho Chang in 1991 as an entry to *Japan Architect*
magazine's annual Shinkenchiku Residential Design
Competition, Vertical Glass House was first realized
in three dimensions in 2013, when the West Bund
Biennale of Architecture and Contemporary Art in
Shanghai decided to construct it as a permanent
pavilion. Conceived as an urban housing prototype
and a comment on the notion of transparency, it offers
a critique of 'Modernist transparency in horizontality':
of glass buildings and homes that open up to their
environment and offer their users little privacy.

Essentially, Vertical Glass House is an upended
Modernist icon. The four-storey residence has enclosed
walls, but a transparent roof and composite tempered
glass floors. The floor slabs extend beyond the shell
of the house and are lit from within. Cast in solid
concrete, the exterior walls have a rough wood
formwork, whereas the interior walls are smooth
in finish. A single, central steel post and steel beams
divide the space into quarters. Intended by the West
Bund Biennale to be a guesthouse for visiting architects
and artists, the Vertical Glass House is fitted with
purpose-made furniture.

The 170m² (1,830ft²)
pavilion has a
footprint of only
40m² (430ft²). The
glass floors are lit
at night, giving
the structure a
'glowing' presence
from the exterior.

A spiral staircase links the interior 7cm (2¾in)-thick glass floors (left, above). There is a double-height atrium at top (right).

SHELTER ISLAND
NEW YORK, USA

ARCHITECT:
STAMBERG AFERIAT + ASSOCIATES

The Shelter Island Pavilion is modest in size – it has an area of just 102m^2 (1,100ft^2) – and is an attempt, as its architects explain, to make 'the line that divides art from architecture...transparent'. Colour is an essential element of the design and, following the principals of Newtonian colour theory, the architects chose a palette that 'allows richly-coloured reflected light to pass through translucent walls, suffusing spaces with a delighting glow'. The structure experienced two 'states' in its production, as architect Peter Stamberg explains: 'The skin of the pavilion is multi-wall polycarbonate and corrugated aluminium, some of which is perforated and some is not. In "State I" the aluminum was unpainted. We loved the lightness of the pavilion in that state, it looks like it is about to take flight. The contrast to our model, the Barcelona Pavilion, which is so much about recognizing gravity, is wonderful. We seriously debated whether to paint or not. The decision to paint, thereby creating a "State II", came down to two reasons. The first relates to Mies' pavilion. We felt that painting would make our composition appear to have just alighted, more related to the gravity in Barcelona than something about to take flight.'

In addition to referencing the Barcelona Pavilion by Ludwig Mies van der Rohe (1929), the architects drew on other icons of Modernist design, including Le Corbusier's Notre-Dame du Haut in Ronchamp, France (1954) and Marcel Breuer's Wassily Chair (1926), as sources of inspiration. Using 'common materials...rendered striking in usage, pigment choice and detailing', the architects created an unexpected, sculptural pavilion on the 5,260m^2 (56,618ft^2) site.

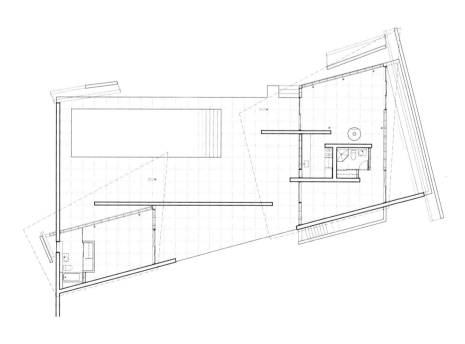

LIVE / WORK / PLAY

The building is
essentially formed
of two 'pavilions',
the design of
which incorporates
translucent double-
polycarbonate walls
to allow light into
each structure.

AIR FRAME PAVILION

BEL AIR
LOS ANGELES, USA

ARCHITECT:
RIOS CLEMENTI HALE STUDIOS

The pavilion has a structural steel frame, motorized glass walls and a windscreen. Fibre optic lighting has been used inside.

The Air Frame Pavilion is a 60m² (646ft²) poolside addition to a three-storey house (designed in 2000 by Gwahtmey Siegel Kaufman Architects). Conceived in response to the client's request for a 'back garden room' the steel-skinned pavilion, with its retractable glass walls, provides 180-degree views of the Pacific Ocean and Los Angeles Basin without obstructing the outlook from the existing residence. There is also a viewing deck on top of the structure. The architects compare their design to a 'high performance vehicle', in part because they have integrated elements like a heating and sound system and electrically operated glass walls, all of which can be controlled using a touch-screen. The architects also designed the central 'fire table' for the pavilion, and selected the other furniture that it houses. The architects explain, 'Conceived as sculpture, Air Frame Pavilion was designed and crafted with rigorous precision to allow views from within the pavilion to be the dominant experience rather than the architecture itself.'

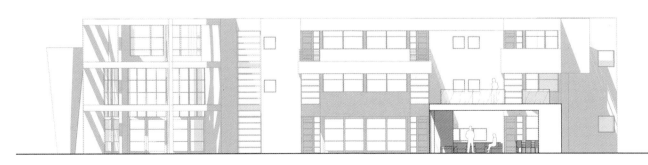

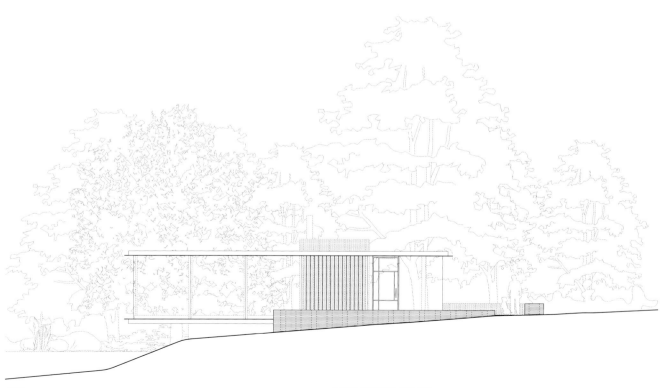

LIVE / WORK / PLAY

SOMERSBY, AUSTRALIA

ARCHITECT:
MATTHEW WOODWARD

The Wirra Willa
pavilion, which takes
its name from the
indigenous word for
green tree, expounds
a relationship to
water, both inside
and out.

The Wirra Willa glass pavilion by the architect Matthew Woodward is, in his own words, 'Miesian inspired', with Mies van der Rohe's Farnsworth House, designed in 1945 and constructed in the city of Plano in Illinois in 1951, being a specific influence. Located on private land that had originally been used as a citrus fruit orchard and which is 32 hectares (79 acres) in area, the structure is cantilevered over a natural spring-fed dam. In keeping with Mies van der Rohe's principles of design, Matthew Woodward explains, 'Simplicity is essential to the success of the project. The approach was to maintain simplicity through each stage of the design process in order to create an elegant, unobtrusive incision into the landscape setting that allows for both prospect and refuge.' Orientated to the northeast, the pavilion has a flexible design, and can be used for multiple functions, with it serving not only as a space in which the surrounding natural area can be appreciated but also as a guesthouse, which includes a bedroom, seating area and small indoor pool. The building comprises two bisecting rectangular blocks, one made of composite steel, concrete and glass, and the other clad in sandstone. A 'rationalized grid' system was used to lay out out the $72m^2$ ($775ft^2$) structure. A further $36m^2$ ($388ft^2$) of external courtyard space allows users to fully enjoy the natural setting.

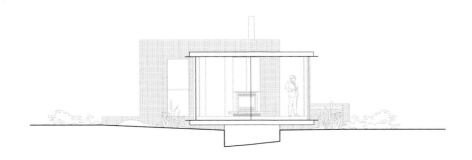

HOJO-AN

SHIMOGAMO JINJA SHRINE
KYOTO, JAPAN

ARCHITECT:
KENGO KUMA

Magnets were
positioned on the
cedar latticework
to hold the plastic
sheets in place,
which could easily
be removed before
the structure
was dismantled
and relocated.

The Japanese author Kamo no Chōmei (1155–1216) lived as a recluse in a tiny hut, an experience that he recorded in his *Hōjōki* (*An Account of a Ten-Foot-Square Hut*; 1212). Drawing on the Buddhist concept of impermanence or *mujo* in his essay, his hut has been described as a prototype for the design of compact housing within Japan. Eight hundred years later, Kengo Kuma (see also pages 268–69) aimed to reconstruct this house using modern methods within the precinct of the Shimogamo Jinja Shrine, a Shinto sanctuary in the city of Kyoto that dates back to the seventh century. Called Hojo-an, the title refers to the scale of the work, the word *hojo* meaning a small cottage approximately 3m² (10ft²) in size. Employing ETFE sheets, which can be removed and rolled up, the structure is portable. Cedar strips combined with powerful magnets were used to create a 'kind of tensegrity structure' which, when combined into a single unit, forms a 'hard box'.

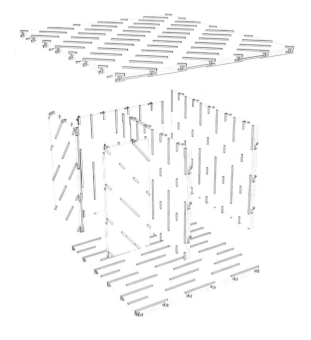

OARE PAVILION

ARCHITECT:
I. M. PEI

Located in Wiltshire, Oare House and its extensive grounds form the site of one of I. M. Pei's smallest realizations, a 289m² (3,110ft²) pavilion, which, like the garden follies of eighteenth-century Europe, has the purpose of providing picturesque views of the surrounding landscape and a space in which to receive guests. The 1999 commission was inspired when Tessa Keswick (wife of Henry Keswick, Chairman of Jardine Matheson Holdings) visited his Miho Museum in Shiragaki in Japan and, on appreciating its design, asked him to make a pavilion for her family home. The architect explains, 'The structure is an octagon 13 × 13m.... You enter the pavilion from below. There is a square opening in the center and you go up steps into the space. You have a 360-degree view of the property, which is very beautiful. The structural frame was designed with the assistance of Leslie Robertson, who also collaborated with me on the Bank of China in Beijing and the Miho Bridge.' In 2010 the architect received a Royal Gold Medal from RIBA for his design. He also received recognition from The Georgian Group that year for the structure, with the English charity stating: 'This striking building, the only one in the United Kingdom by the Chinese-American architect I. M. Pei, punctuates the view from Oare House to the Wiltshire Downs beyond and serves both as an eye-catcher and a comfortable living space-cum-function room. Given that the site is 400 yards from the main house, a fairly large building was needed to perform these two roles. This could have led to an overpowering intervention, but this building is light, airy and ethereal – bravely contemporary in its design but also entirely harmonious in its setting.'

I. M. Pei displays
sensitivity to
the history of
the English garden
'folly' in this
design, here
composed within
an octagonal plan.

HOUSE OF VISION

TOKYO, JAPAN

**ARCHITECT:
HIROSHI SUGIMOTO**

Hiroshi Sugimoto (see also pages 242–45) recently wrote: 'I...am an anachronist: rather than live at the 'cutting edge' of the contemporary, I feel more at ease in the absent past.' This can be seen in his House of Vision, which is based on the aesthetics of the tea house but uses a combination of traditional methods and new technologies in its realization. He created a selection of objects to be used within, including his Five Elements Stool, inspired by the form of the Buddhist pagoda. The 'house' has a roof in rusted galvanized iron, which is covered with tiles produced in the city of Nara. The fence that borders the structure is made from Chinese bamboo brooms. Sugimoto combines disparate elements in this design, including an antique wood grill frame dating from the eighth century, stepping stones from the foothills of Mount Fuji and optical glass, a substance he has used in previous works, including his 2002 Go-Oh Shrine on Naoshima Island.

The project was included in 'House Vision', an exhibition curated by Kenya Hara, which envisaged the future of housing in Japan. Designs by architects Shigeru Ban and Toyo Ito were also featured.

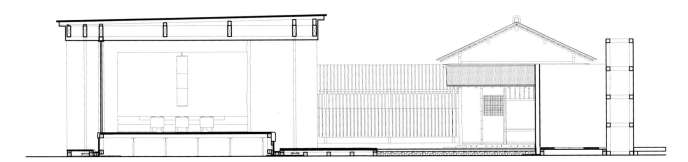

UTSUNOMIYA, JAPAN

ARCHITECT:
TOYO ITO

Toyo Ito was the lead architect and 'curator' of the Sumika project, which also included designs by Sou Fujimoto (pages 44–47), Terunobu Fujimori (pages 240–41) and Taira Nishizawa. Sponsored by Tokyo Gas, the architects were asked to design contemporary and minimalist houses or structures that could be heated by this energy source. The central element of the project was Ito's pavilion, which served as a gathering place and information centre. The Pritzker-prizewinning architect employed laminated lumber within a geometric system supported by four columns, which spread out to form the four walls that encased the 81 m^2 (872 ft^2) structure. Covered with waterproof seamless fibre-reinforced plastic (FRP) and glass, its design gave the impression of fragility, with the angled glass panels collectively taking on the appearance of shattered glass. The architect explains: 'This whole structure symbolizes the primitive living space "Sumika" with simple facilities, creating the image of trees growing and branching overhead.'

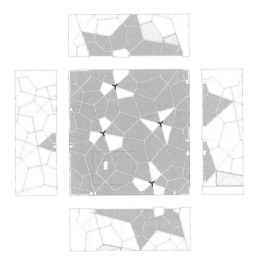

Explaining this project in terms of the form of trees and branches, Toyo Ito returns to a recurring theme in his work: that of artificial or man-made structures that reference nature.

The three skylights above each column and the structure's glass walls allow light to flood into the building.

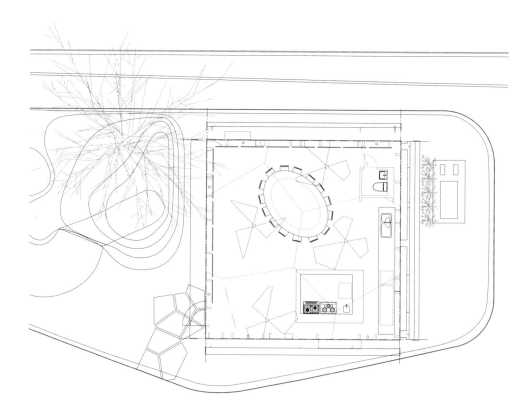

LIVE / WORK / PLAY

AMSTERDAM, THE NETHERLANDS

ARCHITECTS:
BUREAU LADA / DHL ARCHITECTURE

LIVE / WORK / PLAY

Covered completely
in mirrors, the
structure, with its
internal courtyard,
was initially
designed to be 100m²
(1,075ft²) in size.

Designed by the Dutch architect and urbanist Daniëlle Huls of Bureau LADA and the Croatian-Dutch architect Lada Hršak of DHL Architecture, Archive was one of eight winning entries for a competition organized by the Stichting Nieuw en Meer (New and More Foundation) in The Netherlands to create an innovative and functional artist's studio. The designs were constructed at a scale of 1:2, and installed in the foundation's 3.7-hectare (9-acre) site in Amsterdam in 2009. Of the structure the architects explain, 'From the outside, the building is camouflaged with mirrors; it reflects the surroundings, negating its own existence. The large cabinet doors are almost invisible and the entrance must be discovered. The archive's interior has a warm soft core, and is fitted with wooden shelves and "shaker" hooks. It is an uninterrupted space, where the artist can walk around and around, endlessly roaming through their orderly labyrinth – it is a hard disc for the creative mind!'

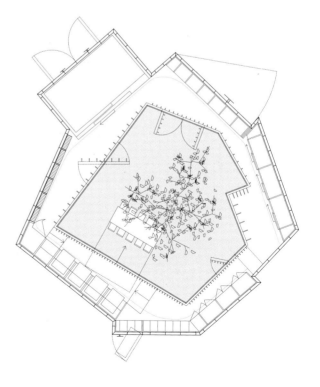

BRUSSELS, BELGIUM

ARCHITECT:
ROTOR

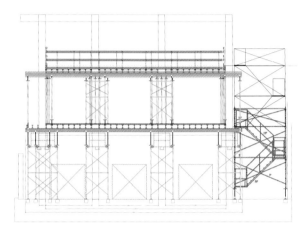

In addition to
serving as the
architects' studio
for a year, the
building also housed
exhibitions and
performances from
invited artists.

Rotor is a non-profit organization based in Brussels that describes itself as 'a platform for the endorsement of industrial waste re-use'. More specifically, they reach out to 'producers of "interesting" waste and potential re-users from the field of industry, design or architecture' with whom to collaborate. In 2006 the group constructed its own office in the city, on a site that had been slated for future redevelopment. Although they did not seek or obtain planning consent, having attained permission from the owner of the site to build there – on the provision that the ground level was left free for parking – Rotor constructed a 60m^2 (646ft^2) structure with a 60m^2 (646ft^2) terrace. On site for just one year, the office, which the architects likened to a 'parasite', was built using 'a rejected lot of plastic film, old exhibition material and transparent sailcloth for the windows, EVA1 foam to insulate the roof, plastic van cladding as terrace paving and materials on loan from building firms for the structure: props, struts and formwork beams'. Highlighting not only the issue of waste in architecture but also that of unused land in cities, RDF181 represented what Rotor principal Maarten Gielen calls 'legal squatting'. The fact that it served as the firm's office, rather than just making a statement about architecture and urban life, makes the suspended volume all the more interesting.

KUNSHAN, CHINA

**ARCHITECT:
VECTOR ARCHITECTS**

The main purposes
of this contemporary,
minimal building
are quite modest:
to collect, process
and store the
farm's harvest.

Located on an 'eco-farm' near Yangcheng Lake, near the city of Kunshan, the Harvest Pavilion was the first of four small-scale public buildings planned for construction in the area. A clubhouse, botanical showroom and information centre were also part of the scheme. The site is described as 'vast, flat and wide open to the sky', to which the architects responded by conceiving a light, horizontal design with a cantilevered roof on all four sides, albeit of different depths. Vertical laminated bamboo louvres over full-height glass walls and pivoting glass doors assure the transparency of the design. In warm weather the doors can be opened up entirely, the result being that 'the indoor space is literally stretched out into the farmland'. Built for the Kunshan City Investment Company, the 150m^2 (1,615ft^2) pavilion has a steel structure and makes use of foam aluminium, cast-in-place concrete, laminated bamboo and glass, among other materials.

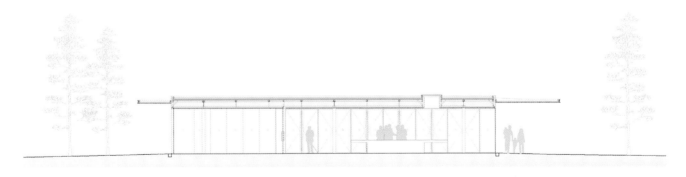

CENTRE POMPIDOU-METZ
PARIS, FRANCE

ARCHITECT:
SHIGERU BAN

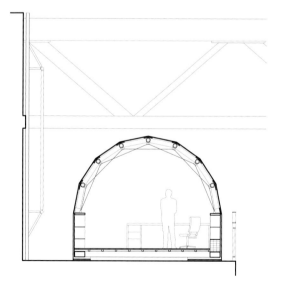

After winning the competition to design the Centre Pompidou-Metz in Paris (a sister institution to the Centre Pompidou, which was conceived by Richard Rogers and Renzo Piano in 1977), Shigeru Ban (see also pages 142–43) sought to create a studio in the city from where he could properly oversee its construction: 'I suggested half jokingly to Bruno Racine, the President of the Centre Pompidou, "that the agreed design fee is not sufficient for an architectural office from a foreign country like us to rent an office in Paris. So if you could lend us space on the terrace, we can build our temporary office". Racine agreed, and Ban's 115m^2 (1,238ft^2) Temporary Paper Studio was constructed on top of the centre's sixth-floor terrace. With its roof made of titanium dioxide PTFE and standard PTFE, the tubular-shaped office stood out clearly against the metallic structure of the building. The interior was finished with tile carpet, wood deck and Vitra furniture, but Ban's own small office cubicle contained his signature cardboard furniture – a desk and chairs – and other pieces to his own design. Ban explains, 'The tubular form of the structure is obviously related to the design of the Centre Pompidou itself, but that also happens to be the most efficient shape. In the original design of Piano and Rogers, they proposed having some temporary structures in or around the building – on the parvis, for example. It was necessary to get the permission of Renzo Piano for this design and he accepted it quite happily. He told me also that when he and Rogers won the Centre Pompidou project, they created a temporary office on a boat anchored on the banks of the Seine. In a way this temporary office is thus connected to the history of the Centre Pompidou. Piano warned me though that it is not a good idea to be too close to the client. He was right.'

The structure
comprised several
areas, including a
lobby, meeting room,
work space, a workshop
and relaxation zone.

LOS VILOS, CHILE

ARCHITECTS:
FELIPE ASSADI ARCHITECTS

Plans (below) show
how the pavilion
(above, opposite),
conceived as a single
work, appears as
a 'dissected bar'.

Located in Los Vilos, a coastal town 224km (140 miles) north of Santiago, this pavilion was developed by the architects to meet a very specific set of conditions. Part of a larger project, which also includes a house and an artist's studio, all situated on the Bahía Azul, the programme involves the provision of buildings to house a sauna, gym, bathrooms and a caretaker's house, all next to tennis courts. The scheme resolves the complexities of relating the structures to one another by forming a 'bar' divided by three 'cuts', which differentiate each space according to its function. Each building has been rotated slightly in relation to its neighbour. The continuous vertical wood cladding that leads up to the angled single-sloped roofs assures the legibility of the divided complex as a single work of architecture. Comparing this plan to a 'dissection' of the original bar form, which can be seen in the accompanying house and artist's studio, the architects state that the structure remains enough in one piece to 'remember its initial state prior to the cuts we made'. In plan, the pavilion brings to mind a child's train set seen from above, with wagons of different lengths turned at slightly varied angles.

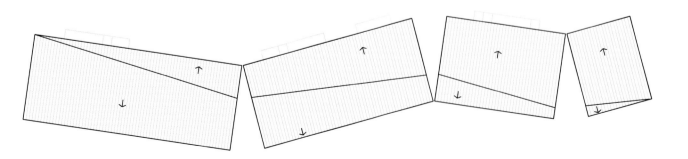

LIVE / WORK / PLAY

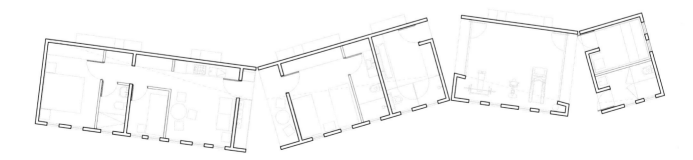

FELIPE ASSADI ARCHITECTS

LIVE / WORK / PLAY

OXFORD, UK

**ARCHITECT:
JOHN PAWSON**

The minimalist simplicity of the design of this 203m² (2,185ft²) pavilion is a signature element in the work of John Pawson.

John Pawson's (see also pages 94–95) 1996 visual essay 'Minimum' identified him as a leading light of an apparently reductive or 'minimalist' trend in contemporary architecture. The Martyrs Pavilion, a cricket pavilion made for St Edward's School in Oxford, is just that, made up essentially from a plinth and a roof with cantilevered overhangs that provide shelter from sun and rain. Positioned on a grass-covered mound overlooking the pitch, the structure expresses an elegant simplicity that is very much in keeping with the architect's style. Pawson explains, 'Given the spare nature of the overall form, the use of marble for the roof and plinth edges becomes a significant gesture, adding a little material richness and setting up a defining dialogue with the vertical oak panels cladding the walls.' The single-storey structure includes a meeting /function room, changing rooms, shower facilities and a kitchen. The external walls were built using fair-faced blocks and clad on the outside with European oak. The perimeter of the veranda is covered in natural marble, while Marmi marble was used for the roof. The pavilion was the winner of the Oxfordshire Preservation Trust Award in 2010.

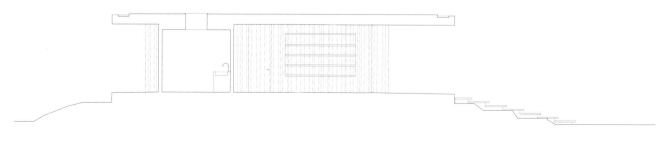

BEETLE'S HOUSE

V&A MUSEUM
LONDON, UK

ARCHITECT:
TERUNOBU FUJIMORI

A 4m² (43ft²) structure erected within London's V&A Museum, Terunobu Fujimori's Beetle's House was one of seven structures included in the exhibition '1:1 Architects Build Small Spaces', which ran from 15 June to 30 August in 2010. In addition to Beetle's House, other proposals included works by the architects Sou Fujimoto (pages 44–47) and Studio Mumbai (pages 252–53). A Professor Emeritus at the University of Tokyo's Institute of Industrial Science, Fujimori is well known for his structures that involve the subtle modification of traditional Japanese architecture. In Japan he has conceived a number of tea houses, some of which – like Beetle's House – are elevated high above ground. He writes: 'In the architectural history of the world, the Japanese tea house is the one and only example of a small building that is acknowledged as a building type. Given this history, I made a tea house for drinking tea in the United Kingdom. After the black tea, charcoal was used for the inside and outside finishes.' Fujimori had intended for Beetle's House to be suspended from the ceiling but in the end chose legs for supports. Nonetheless it remains very much in keeping with his whimsical style and reinterpretation of Japanese architecture, an approach that is particularly refreshing within the Western context in which it was displayed.

The charred black wood that forms the exterior was chosen for its durability - it is a naturally waterproof and pestproof material - and also features in the interior, in a carefully arranged pattern conceived by the architect.

**VENICE ARCHITECTURE BIENNALE
VENICE, ITALY**

**ARCHITECT:
HIROSHI SUGIMOTO**

Best known for his work as a photographer, Hiroshi Sugimoto (see also pages 218-19) has also designed a number of exhibition spaces and small structures. His Glass Tea House Mondrian was installed in the gardens of the island of San Giorgio Maggiore in Venice during the 2014 Architecture Biennale, and refers to the elevation of the act of preparing tea to an art, a tradition that has been practised by the Japanese since the sixteenth century. 'The tea ceremony,' he explains, 'encompasses all the individual arts of the West. In addition to painting and dance, there is sculpture (in the shape of the porcelain bowl), music (in the sound of the water on the boil) and architecture (in the form of the tea ceremony arbor). These disparate elements intertwine, coalescing to form a single, perfect whole.' The reference to Mondrian comes through Sugimoto's desire to communicate all of this in the form of abstraction. He affirms too that Sen no Rikyū – a historical figure who perfected the tea ceremony and whose placement of stones in the garden or composed flat wall surfaces at Taian, a sixteenth-century tea room which still stands near Kyoto, could be said to be 'abstraction' – was a source of inspiration. Rather than the traditional small, closed structures in which tea ceremonies commonly take place, Sugimoto chose to make his form in glass. Set within a rectangular basin, the structure is surrounded by a bamboo barrier and carefully positioned stones, which allow visitors to reach the inner sanctum of this installation via a circuitous route.

Offering a space for contemplation and privacy, the pavilion comprised two main elements: the $5m^3$ ($176ft^3$) house, in which tea ceremonies could be performed, and the surrounding courtyard, for spectators.

The house can be accessed via staggered wooden landings (above). Visitors can rest in the shelter in the surrounding courtyard (right).

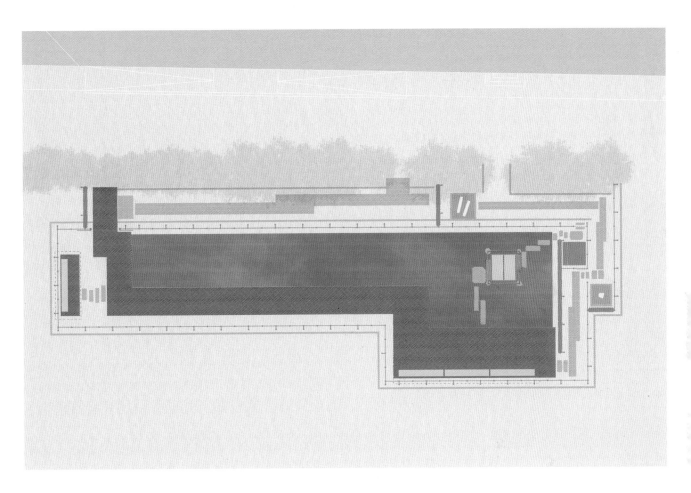

A plan showing the
expansive courtyard
and mosaic-tiled pool
in which the house
was positioned.

SHELTER

**DESIGN MIAMI
MIAMI, USA**

**ARCHITECT:
FORMLESSFINDER**

Since 2008, Design Miami has 'commissioned emerging architecture practices to design unique architectural experiences at the fair'. In 2013, the organizers invited the young New York practice formlessfinder, headed by Garrett Ricciardi and Julian Rose, to make a structure that would offer shelter and seating for visitors to the event. The architects take a radical approach to sustainability and the importance of the site. They seek 'to exploit found conditions, to use what already exists. A material like bamboo may scream sustainable, but as often as not it is shipped halfway around the world to the construction site.... [We] would rather build with the dust, dirt, and gravel already there.' In Miami, the architects focused on the ubiquity of sand in the city, using a large pile of this material together with a lightweight aluminium roof to shape the pavilion. The roof and the space it created were a commentary on the numerous cantilevered canopies with no walls found in Miami, offering shelter from the weather and easy access. This combination relates to their efforts to create 'an architecture that can go from nothing to something and back again'. A retaining wall limited the spread of the sand pile near the entrance to the fair. Aluminium fins passing through the plywood surface of the wall took advantage of the thermal mass of the sand, keeping the seating area cool.

```
The sand pile was a
stabilizing element
for the cantilevered
roof, which itself
was made from CNC-
machined aluminium
and finished with a
protective lustre.
```

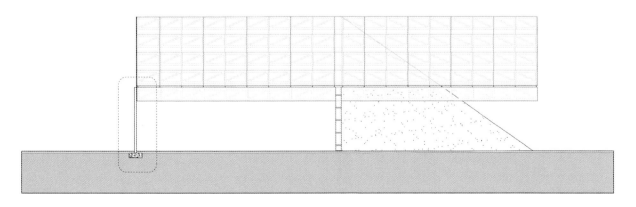

NATIONAL MUSEUM OF MODERN ART
TOKYO, JAPAN

ARCHITECT:
STUDIO MUMBAI

Conceived as three open-air wooden structures or huts, the MOMAT pavilion, designed for the National Museum of Modern Art in Tokyo, is one of a number of innovative projects produced by the Indian practice Studio Mumbai. Others include their In-Between Architecture pavilion for the '1:1 Architects Build Small Spaces' exhibition at London's Victoria and Albert Museum in 2010. The intention of the installation in Tokyo was to provide visitors with a place to rest in the museum's front garden while its main gallery was closed for refurbishment. The architects brought craftsmen with them from Mumbai to execute the construction on site. The design concept involved a 'fusion' of the huts that were made and used in Japan after the Second World War and the designs found in the architecture of rural Indian villages. Each with its own name – the Pavilion Window, Pavilion Tower and Pavilion Swing – the huts sought to make uncertain the boundaries between inside and outside.

The 'bird trees'
positioned between
the huts are made
from bamboo rods
topped with a gridded
mesh, and refer to
structures that are
typically used in
Udaipur, Rajasthan,
to attract wildlife.

SHANGHAI, CHINA

ARCHITECT:
B+H ARCHITECTS

Providing shelter
for users of the
park, the pavilion's
wooden cladding
was arranged in a
'scattered' pattern,
to make its form
'dissolve' into its
natural setting.

B+H Architects, a Canadian firm that also has studios in China, India and the United Arab Emirates, is responsible for acclaimed buildings such as the Hong Kong New World Tower (2002) and the Great Wall Tower (2008), both in Shanghai. In 2012 the firm designed the Butterfly Pavilion for the Daning Lingshi Park in Shanghai's downtown district of Zhabei. Comprising 68 hectares (186 acres) in total, the park is the largest green space in an area mainly overrun by urban development. The pavilion was conceived by B+H as a gift to the city in return for the many commissions that the architects have received since opening an office there in 1992. The pavilion is something of a 'folly', in the eighteenth-century European sense of the term – an essentially decorative structure that one might expect to see in the expansive gardens in the grand homes of England and France – but in this instance made from wood and displaying an unconventional profile, which nonetheless is intentionally related to a number of local traditions or sources of inspiration (the forms of butterfly cocoons, Chinese lanterns and traditional theatre, for example). One of the largest architecture, interior design and urban planning firms in the world, B+H indulges here in a contrast between the scope of its own projects and their modernist design and an attempt to bring together the history, traditions and materials of China.

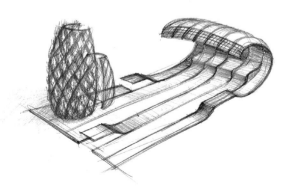

B+H ARCHITECTS

WINNIPEG, CANADA

**ARCHITECT:
KEVIN ERICKSON**

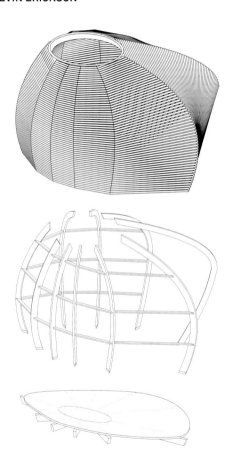

A winner of the Warming Huts 2012 international art and architecture competition, the Rope Pavilion was built on Winnipeg's Red river, which freezes over in winter (becoming 'the world's longest naturally frozen skating trail'). Other architects, including Antoine Predock (Apparition hut, 2010), Frank O. Gehry (Five-Hole hut, 2012) and Michael Rojkind (Hybrid Hut, 2015; pages 262–63) have also seen their designs realized here. The exterior – made from unmanila rope, a synthetic, tan-coloured alternative to manila, which resists the cold – was attached to a dome-like structure made from birch. The architect, Kevin Erickson, is principal of KNEstudio in New York and Assistant Professor at the School of Architecture at the University of Illinois, and worked with Arup in New York to engineer the structure. Numerous full-scale prototypes and models were created and tested before its implementation. Gaps between the rope allow light to enter into the space, but it has only two significant openings, one the central oculus at top and the other the entrance, where the rope has the appearance of having been lifted and pulled back to provide access.

An exploded axonometric
drawing (above) shows
the relatively simple
form of the asymmetric
pavilion (opposite,
overleaf).

KEVIN ERICKSON

WEBB CHAPEL PARK PAVILION

WEBB CHAPEL PARK
DALLAS, USA

ARCHITECT:
STUDIO JOSEPH

In 2002 the Dallas Department of Parks and Recreation initiated a long-term strategic development plan leading to the renovation, design and construction of a number of shelters and pavilions in the city's parks. Designed by Studio Joseph, the Webb Chapel Park Pavilion was relocated to a site next to a playground and football pitch, providing seating and shade for the users of these recreational grounds. The cantilevered poured-in-place concrete structure is positioned on three structural supports. It has a passive cooling system integrated into the design, which offers respite from the hot Texan climate. Four pyramidal voids in the roof encourage natural ventilation, drawing in convection breezes generated by temperature differences, benefiting the seating area below. The architects write: 'The solution asserts pure geometry to simultaneously achieve bold form and function. A concrete canopy of exaggerated depth enables a simple structure with minimal visible supports to create virtually seamless views of the surrounding site.'

The pavilion was
inspired by the
traditional Mexican
palapa, a dwelling
without walls
that draws hot air
upwards, leaving the
area beneath cool.

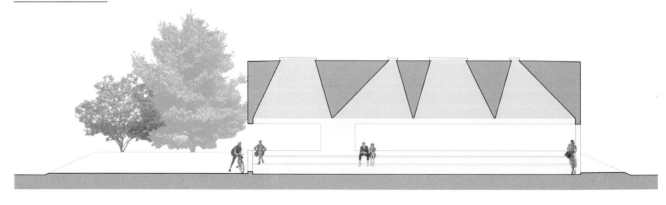

HYBRID HUT

WINNIPEG, CANADA

ARCHITECT:
ROJKIND ARQUITECTOS

Placing an emphasis on 'digital design and local fabrication' in his work, in 2014 the architect Michel Rojkind made a pavilion for Warming Huts, an annual competition held in the city of Winnipeg, which calls on architects and artists to design shelters for the city's Red river as it freezes over during winter. Rojkind relied on computer-assisted design for his structure but also acknowledged Canada's wood industry – in particular the production of laminated wood beams – in his choice of materials. He also investigated the possibility of using reclaimed wood and local craft techniques. As the architect explains, 'Understanding its parts, once the digitally designed structure was assembled and put in place, we arrived in Winnipeg to build the rest of the pavilion with a local team. Leaving the tree bark on the outside, the Hybrid Hut allows a contrast between the smooth inside and the texturized pieces on the outside.' The Hut occupied an area of 75m^2 (807ft^2). Its unusual form readily evokes the kind of 'hybrid' that its title implies – appearing almost as a primitive creature that has been brought to life using 3D technology.

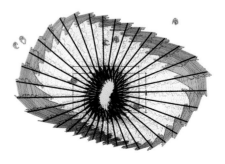

263

LONG ISLAND CITY
NEW YORK, USA

ARCHITECT:
THE LIVING

The 13m (42ft)-high
tower was made from a
total of ten thousand
compostable bricks.

Winner of the fifteenth Young Architects Program at MoMA PS1 in Long Island City, Hy-Fi was designed by The Living founder David Benjamin and installed in the courtyard of the institution in 2014. The structure was made from lightweight organic bricks stacked to form a tubular tower, a shape made for the purpose of creating an upward air current that would cool the interior. A reflective film made by 3M Design was placed on the upper part of the tower to bring light into the interior. Benjamin states, 'Our structure uses biological technologies combined with cutting-edge computation and engineering to create new building materials, a new method of bio-design, and a structure for MoMA PS1 that is 100% grown and 100% compostable.' The bricks, made from elements such as corn stalks and 'specially developed living root structures', eventually became compost. A local non-profit organization, Build It Green Compost, was called on to process the building materials after the installation, which they distributed to community gardens in Queens. Benjamin's 'green' vision of architecture is a clear contrast to the steel and glass towers of nearby Manhattan. It was also very carefully thought out, with Arup commissioned as the structural engineers and Bruce Mau Design as the 'branding collaborator'. Benjamin is an Assistant Professor at Columbia University Graduate School of Architecture, Planning and Preservation and founder of design studio The Living.

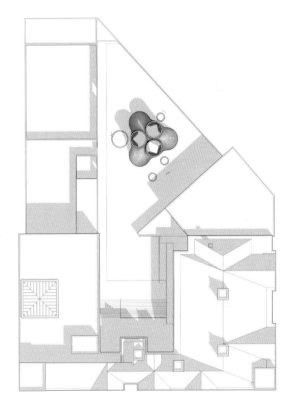

CASA UMBRELLA

**MILAN TRIENNALE
MILAN, ITALY**

**ARCHITECT:
KENGO KUMA**

This 15m² (160ft²) 'temporary house' was designed
by Kengo Kuma (see also pages 214–15) for the
exhibition 'Casa Per Tutti' during the Milan Triennale
in 2008. Kuma sought to use materials that were
commonly available in his proposal, which brought
to mind the ubiquity of the umbrella – lightweight, easy
to carry and offering protection against the elements.
As the architect explains, 'This "Casa Umbrella" is
composed of each triangle on a regular icosahedron
[being] replaced by an umbrella. A triangle created
by the bones of the umbrella is utilized as a truss
structure, and every single detail is...[an adaptation
of the features of the] umbrella.' The umbrellas are
joined together by zips that are more commonly used
in diving suits, the configuration of which allowed for
openings to be made at any point where the umbrellas
met, simply by undoing the joins. The covering was
a polyester non-woven fabric called Tyvek produced
by DuPont, a material that is easy to sew. Above all,
it is very water resistant. According to the manufacturer,
'Tyvek has a higher strength-to-weight ratio thanpaper,
absorbs little or no moisture, is strong and rip-resistant,
and is made of environmentally responsible material.
Both bright white and silky smooth, Tyvek has a
distinctive look and feel that enhances graphic images
and instantly sets it apart from all other materials.'
The pavilion's title was a play on words: 'casa' meaning
'umbrella' in Japanese and 'home' in Italian.

The structure was
built from fifteen
umbrella bones zipped
together, and had
multiple purposes:
pop-up shelter,
provisional home
and emergency room.

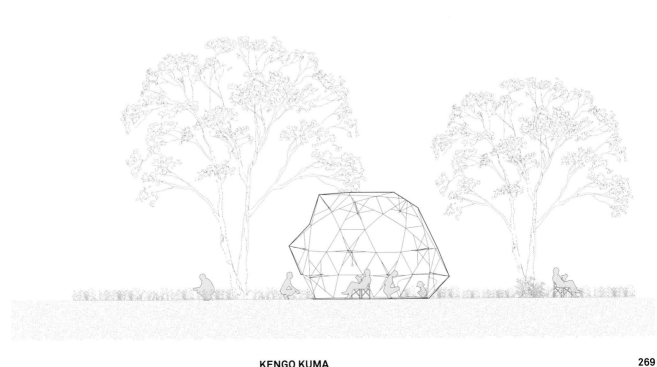

KENGO KUMA

DESIGN MIAMI
MIAMI, USA

ARCHITECT:
SNARKITECTURE

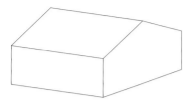 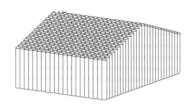 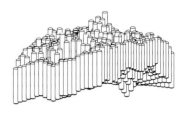

A temporary pavilion made for the entrance of Design Miami 2012, Drift was formed of long, inflatable tubes of white vinyl, bundled together 'to create a topographical landscape in suspension: an ascending mountain above and an excavated cavern below'. Arranged vertically and filling the best part of the entrance courtyard, with the exception of a small central 'skylight' and a few irregular openings, the tubes were hung at varied lengths 'to create areas of circulation and rest for the visitors entering and exiting the structure'. Light filtered between the tubes, and the various openings allowed air to circulate through the structure and provided views of the sky. Suspended above the ground to provide shade, but also extending above the equally white tent erected for the event, Drift provided something of a signal of the presence of a creative event, while also offering a comment on standardized white exhibition tents. The clustering and height variations of the tube configurations also provide this pavilion with an organic feel, in contrast to the materials with which it has been made.

Despite its 'organic' appearance, the architects produced exacting diagrams of each and every tube before the structure was installed.

SAPPORO, JAPAN

ARCHITECT:
HIDEMI NISHIDA

The Fragile Shelter was a small 20m² (215ft²) structure built in a forest near the city of Sapporo in Japan. It was assembled with panels measuring 2 × 2m (7 × 7ft) and designed for ease of transport. Made up of six basic units, the structure was also conceived so that it would be easy to deconstruct and store when not in use. Plastic sheeting usually found in agriculture and timber were the materials from which it was constructed. The architect explains, 'We used materials that are cheap and easy to manipulate, as well as being available everywhere in Japan.' Born in 1986, Hidemi Nishida received a degree in architecture in 2007, but considers himself more an 'environmental artist' than an architect. 'This project is a temporary shelter in the wild winter forest,' he explains. 'It leads people to gather, and a number of events happened there.... This is a cozy base for winter activities.' Emphasizing an area of inquiry that has been quite popular in recent years in Japan, which is to say the origins of the house, Nishida claims of his structure: 'This is a reconfirmation of the beginning of the "house".'

Assembling a simple, light building with plastic sheeting and wood in a remote location, the architect poses the question of how to constitute an effective shelter with the most limited construction means possible.

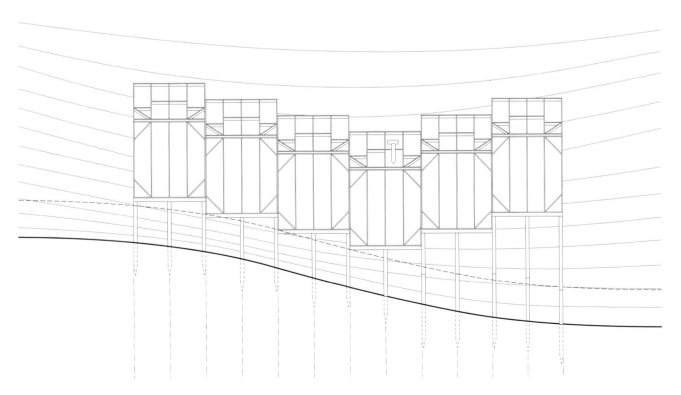

PUERTO ESCONDIDO
OAXACA, MEXICO

ARCHITECT:
FEDERICO RIVERA RIO

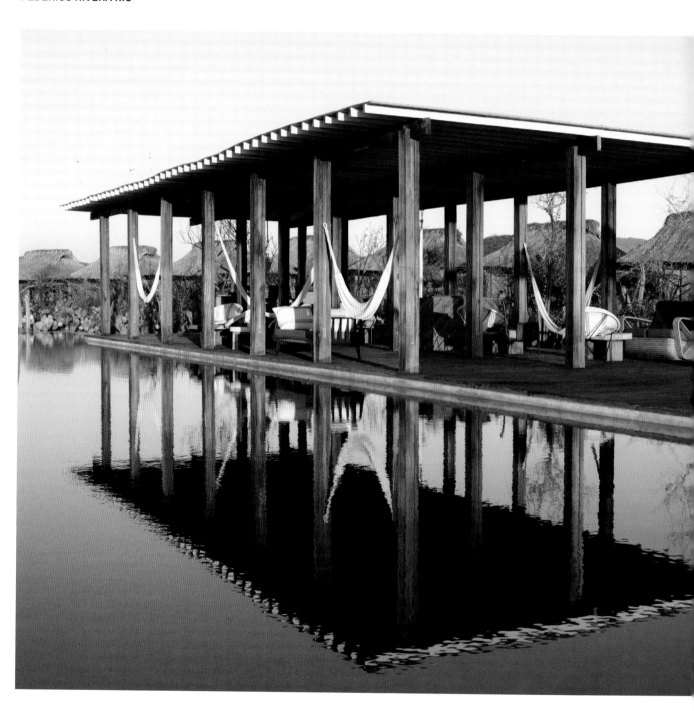

The pavilion provides
shelter for users of the
hotel's swimming pool.

Part of a hotel project located on the southern Pacific coast of Mexico, this pavilion is made largely from Parota wood, with palm used for the roof. The floor is also made from Parota, which has been finished in oil. Located next to the hotel's swimming pool, the structure is 18m (59ft) long, 7m (23ft) wide and 2.7m (9ft) high. The architect explains, 'The main concept of the project is the use of local, ancient, traditional architecture with its ancestral forms and customs, transformed into contemporary architecture with simple lines and geometric rigor. In tropical climes palm-leaf roofs on wooden structures and stone walls remain unbeatable. Their low ecological impact [makes them] a real option for construction. We only use local materials. The design of cross ventilation spaces (despite [the presence of] air conditioners and fans), the use of solar energy to heat, and the use of only reclaimed Parota wood for flooring, furniture and blinds was very important to maintain the sustainable feeling throughout Hotel Escondido.'

Four-Use Pavilion (234–37)
Date: 2014
Location: Los Vilos, Chile
Architect: Felipe Assadi
Architects: Felipe Assadi,
Francisca Pulido and
Alejandra Araya
Area: 23m² (248ft²)

Fragile Shelter (274–77)
Date: 2011
Location: Sapporo, Japan
Architect: Hidemi Nishida
Area: 20m² (215ft²)

**Glass Tea House Mondrian
(242–45)**
Date: 2014
Location: Venice, Italy
Architect: Hiroshi Sugimoto
Client: Le Stanze del Vetro
(Fondazione Cini and
Pentagram Stiftung)
Area: 40m² (430ft²)

Golden Moon (102–05)
Date: 2012
Location: Hong Kong, China
Architect: LEAD; Kristof Crolla
and Adam Fingrut
Client: (Sponsor) Lee Kum Kee
Area: 360m² (3,875ft²)

Golden Workshop (136–37)
Date: 2012
Location: Münster, Germany
Architect: modulorbeat; Marc
Günnewig and Jan Kampshoff
Client: LWL State Museum for
Art and Art History
Area: 95m² (1,023ft²)

Groovy Spiral (70–71)
Date: 2013
Location: London, UK
Artist: Dan Graham
Area: 33m² (355ft²)

The Hangar (172–73)
Date: 2009
Location: New South
Wales, Australia
Architect: Peter Stutchbury
Client: Cessnock Aerodrome
Area: 1,886m² (20,300ft²)

Harvest Pavilion (228–31)
Date: 2012
Location: Kunshan, China
Architect: Vector
Architects; Feng Xu
Client: Kunshan City
Investment Company
Area: 150m² (1,615ft²)

Hojo-an (214–15)
Date: 2012
Location: Kyoto, Japan
Architects: Kengo Kuma
Area: 9m² (97ft²)

**Hotel Escondido Pavilion
(278–79)**
Date: 2013
Location: Puerto Escondido,
Oaxaca, Mexico
Architect: Federico Rivera Rio
Client: Hotel Escondio, Oaxaca
Area: 126m² (1,356ft²)

House of Vision (218–19)
Date: 2013
Location: Tokyo, Japan
Architect: Hiroshi Sugimoto
Area: 256m² (2,756ft²)

Hy-Fi (264–67)
Date: 2014
Location: Long Island City, New
York, USA
Architect: The Living; David
Benjamin
Client: MoMA PS1 / Young
Architects Program (YAP)
Area: 81m² (872ft²)

Hybrid Hut (262–63)
Date: 2014
Location: Winnipeg, Canada
Architect: Rojkind
Arquitectos; Michel Rojkind
Client: Warming Huts
International Design
Competition
Area: 75m² (807ft²)

Jellyfish Theatre (176–79)
Date: 2010
Location: London, UK
Architects: Martin Kaltwasser
and Folke Köebberling
Client: The Red Room Theatre
and Film Company / The
Architecture Foundation
Area: 246m² (2,648ft²)

The Lantern (62–65)
Date: 2008
Location: Sandnes, Norway
Architect: AWP /
AtelierOslo; Marc Armengaud,
Matthias Armengaud and
Alessandrea Cianchetta
Client: City of Sandnes
Area: 140m² (1,507ft²)

League of Shadows (42–43)
Date: 2012
Location: Los Angeles,
California, USA
Architect:
P-A-T-T-E-R-N-S; Marcelo
Spina and Georgina Huljich
Client: Southern California
Institute of Architecture
Area: 90m² (969ft²)

Living Pavilion (114–15)
Date: 2010
Location: Governors Island,
New York, USA
Architect: Behin Ha; Behrang
Behin and Ann Ha
Client: FIGMENT, ENYA
and SEAoNY)
Area: 54m² (581ft²)

**London 2012 BMW Group
Pavilion (144–45)**
Date: 2012
Location: London, UK
Architect: Serie
Architects; Christopher Lee
Client: BMW (AG)
Area: 1,600m² (17,222ft²)

Margaret Whitlam Pavilion (182–83)
Date: 2013
Location: Canberra, Australia
Architect: Tonkin Zulaikha Greer
Architects; Peter Tonkin, John
Chesterman, Juliane Wolter,
Wolfgang Ripberger, Elizabeth
Muir and Trina Day
Client: ACT Government
Area: 24m² (258ft²)

Marseille Vieux Port Pavilion (188–89)
Date: 2013
Location: Marseille, France
Architect: Foster + Partners;
Norman Foster and Spencer
de Grey
Client: MPM, Marseille
Provence Metropole
Area: 1,012m² (10,893ft²)

Martyrs Pavilion (238–39)
Date: 2009
Location: Oxford, UK
Architect: John Pawson
Client: St Edward's School
Area: 24m² (258ft²)

Mobile Art Pavilion for Chanel (146–47)
Date: 2007–14
Location: Hong Kong, China;
Tokyo, Japan; New York, USA;
Paris, France
Architect: Zaha Hadid Architects
Client: Chanel, Karl Lagerfeld
Area: 700m² (7,535ft²)

MOMAT Pavilion (252–53)
Date: 2012
Location: Tokyo, Japan
Architect: Studio Mumbai;
Bijoy Jain
Client: National Museum
of Modern Art (MOMAT)
Area: 36m² (387ft²)

NO99 Straw Theatre (180–81)
Date: 2011
Location: Talinn, Estonia
Architect: Salto AB; Maarja
Kask, Karli Luik, Ralf Lõoke
Client: Theatre NO99
Area: 440m² (4,736ft²)

Nine Pavilions (24–25)
Date: 2007
Location: Yverdon-les-Bains,
Switzerland
Architect: Localarchitecture
Client: Guggenheim Foundation
and BMW
Area: dimensions variable

Nomiya (36–39)
Date: 2009
Location: Palais de Tokyo, Paris,
France
Architect / Artist: Pascal Grasso
and Laurent Grasso
Client: Palais de Tokyo /
Electrolux
Area: 64m² (690ft²)

Norwegian Wild Reindeer Centre Pavilion (184–87)
Date: 2011
Location: Hjerkinn, Dovre,
Norway
Architect: Snøhetta;
Kjetil Thorsen
Client: Norwegian Wild
Reindeer Foundation
Area: 90m² (969ft²)

Oare Pavilion (216–17)
Date: 2003
Location: Wiltshire, UK
Architect: I. M. Pei
Clients: Henry and
Tessa Keswick
Area: 289m² (3,111ft²)

Pavilion 21 MINI Opera Space (190–93)
Date: 2010
Location: Munich, Germany
Architect: Coop
Himmelb(l)au; Wolf D. Prix,
Volker Killian and Sophie-
Charlotte Grell
Client: The Bavarian State
Opera, Munich, Germany
Area: 430m² (4,628ft²)

Peace Pavilion (94–95)
Date: 2013
Location: London, UK
Architect: Atelier Zündel
Cristea; Irina Cristea and
Grégoire Zündel
Client: ArchTriumph
Area: 20m² (215ft²)

People's Meeting Dome (120–123)
Date: 2012
Location: Allinge, Bornholm,
Denmark
Architects: Benny Jepsen
and Kristoffer Tejlgaard
Client: BL (Denmark's
Public Housing)
Area: 212m² (2,282ft²)

Potters Fields Park Pavilions (26–29)
Date: 2007
Location: London, UK
Architect: DSDHA; Deborah
Saunt and John Zang
Client: More London Ltd
Area: 295m² (3,175ft²)

PUMACity (150–51)
Date: 2008
Location: Alicante, Spain;
Boston, Massachusetts, USA
Architect: LOT-EK; Giuseppe
Lignano and Ada Tolla
Client: PUMA
Area: 1,000m² (10,764ft²)

RDF181 (226–27)
Date: 2006
Location: Brussels, Belgium
Architect: Rotor; Tristan Boniver,
Lionel Devlieger, Maarten Gielen
and Mia Schmallenbach
Area: 60m² (646ft²)

***Red Beacon* (78–79)**
Date: 2010
Location: Shanghai, China
Artist: Arne Quinze
Area: 2,400m² (25,833ft²)

Research Pavilion (118–19)
Date: 2011
Location: Stuttgart, Germany
Architects: ICD / ITKE; Achim
Menges and Jan Knippers
Area: 87m² (936ft²)

**The Roof That Goes Up In
Smoke (40–41)**
Date: 2010
Location: Roosendaal,
The Netherlands
Architect: Overtreders
W; Reinder Bakker and
Hester van Dijk
Client: Schatten van Brabant
Area: 54m² (581ft²)

Rope Pavilion (256–59)
Date: 2012
Location: Winnipeg, Canada
Architect: Kevin Erickson
Client: Warming Huts
International Design
Competition
Area: 9.3m² (100ft²)

**Serpentine Gallery Pavilion
(30–33)**
Date: 2015
Location: London, UK
Architect: SelgasCano;
José Selgas and Lucía Cano
Client: Serpentine Gallery
Area: 264m² (2,842ft²)

**Serpentine Gallery Pavilion
(44–47)**
Date: 2013
Location: London, UK
Architect: Sou Fujimoto
Client: Serpentine Gallery
Area: 357m² (3,843ft²)

**Serpentine Gallery Pavilion
(22–23)**
Date: 2012
Location: London, UK
Architects: Herzog & de Meuron
/ Ai Weiwei
Client: Serpentine Gallery
Area: 660m² (7,104ft²)

Shadow Pavilion (116–17)
Date: 2009
Location: Ann Arbor,
Michigan, USA
Architect: PLY Architecture;
Karl Daubman
Client: University of Michigan
Matthaei Botanical Gardens
Area: 42m² (452ft²)

**Shanghai Corporate Pavilion
(152–55)**
Date: 2010
Location: Shanghai, China
Architect: Atelier FCJZ; Yung
Ho Chang and Zang Feng
Client: Shanghai Guosheng
Group Co. Ltd
Area: 5,000m² (53,820ft²)

**Shelter Island Pavilion
(204–07)**
Date: 2010
Location: Shelter Island,
New York, USA
Architect: Stamberg Aferiat +
Associates; Peter Stamberg
and Paul Aferiat
Area: 102m² (1,098ft²)

Silk Pavilion (124–25)
Date: 2013
Location: Cambridge,
Massachusetts, USA
Architect: MIT Media Lab;
Neri Oxman
Area: 1.5m² (5ft²)

***Sky is the Limit* (72–75)**
Date: 2008
Location: YangYang,
South Korea
Artist: Didier Faustino
Area: 50m² (538ft²)

The Source (140–41)
Date: 2012
Location: Liverpool, UK
Architect / Artist: David Adjaye
/ Doug Aitken
Client: Tate Liverpool / Sky
Arts Ignition
Area: 160m² (1,722ft²)

Stone House (94–95)
Date: 2010
Location: Milan, Italy
Architect: John Pawson
Area: 8m² (86ft²)

Sumika Pavilion (220–23)
Date: 2009
Location: Utsunomiya,
Tochigi Prefecture, Japan
Architect: Toyo Ito
Client: (Sponsor) Tokyo Gas
Area: 81m² (872ft²)

**Temporary Museum (Lake)
(156–57)**
Date: 2010
Location: Heemskerk,
The Netherlands
Architect: Anne Holtrop
Client: Stichting Beeldende
Kunst Manifestatie Heemskerk
Area: 40m² (431ft²)

**Temporary Paper Studio
(232–33)**
Date: 2004
Location: Paris, France
Architects: Shigeru Ban
Area: 50m² (538ft²)

Tent Pile (248–51)
Date: 2013
Location: Miami, Florida, USA
Architect: formlessfinder;
Garrett Ricciardi and
Julian Rose
Client: Design Miami 2013
Area: 40m² (930ft²)

**Thornton Park Community
Pavilion (48–49)**
Date: 2013
Location: North Penrith, New
South Wales, Australia
Architect: MBMO; Morris Bray
and Martin Ollmann
Area: 700m² (7,535ft²)

TKTS Booth (56–59)
Date: 2008
Location: New York, USA
Architects: Perkins Eastman /
Choi Rophia
Client: Times Square Alliance,
Theatre Development Fund,
Coalition for Father Duffy and
City of New York
Area: 79m² (850ft²)

Uchronia (80–81)
Date: 2006
Location: Black Rock City,
Black Rock, Nevada, USA
Artist: Arne Quinze
Client: Lexus
Area: 1,830m² (19,698ft²)

**Underwood Pavilion
(112–13)**
Date: 2014
Location: Muncie, Indiana, USA
Architects: Gernot Riether and
Andrew Wit
Area: 18m² (194ft²)

Upcycling Pavilion (34–35)
Date: 2012
Location: Mexico City, Mexico
Architect: Bunker Arquitectura;
Esteban Suarez
Client: EXPO CIHAC
Area: 300m² (3,229ft²)

Vaulted Willow (86–89)
Date: 2014
Location: Edmonton, Canada
Architect: THEVERYMANY;
Marc Thornes
Client: Edmonton Public
Art, Canada
Area: 6.7m² (72ft²)

**Vistula River Beach Pavilion
(50–53)**
Date: 2013
Location: Warsaw, Poland
Architect: Ponadto Grupa
Projektowa; Aleksandra
Krzywanska, Maja
Matuszewska and Katarzyna
Szpicmacher
Client: Sanitec KOLO
Area: 1500m² (16,14fft²)

VM Pavilion (66–67)
Date: 2011
Location: Oslo, Norway
Architect: Snøhetta; Kjetil
Thorsen
Client: Øyer Invest AS
Area: 180m² (1,938ft²)

**Webb Chapel Park Pavilion
(160–61)**
Date: 2012
Location: Dallas, Texas, USA
Architect: Studio Joseph;
Chris Cooper and Wendy
Evans Joseph
Client: City of Dallas,
Department of Parks
and Recreation
Area: 84m² (903ft²)

Wendy (90–93)
Date: 2012
Location: Long Island City,
New York, USA
Architect: HWKN; Matthias
Hollwich and Marc Kushner
Client: MoMA PS1 and Sheikha
Salama Bint Hamdan Al Nahyan
Foundation and Masdar
Area: 70m² (753ft²)

Whitney Studio (134–35)
Date: 2012
Location: New York, USA
Architect: LOT-EK; Giuseppe
Lignano and Ada Tolla
Client: The Whitney Museum
of American Art
Area: 60m² (646ft²)

Wild Beast Pavilion (194–97)
Date: 2010
Location: Valencia, California,
USA
Architect: HplusF
Architecture; Craig Hodgetts
and Hsin-Ming Fung
Client: California Institute
of the Arts
Area: 228m² (2,453ft²)

Wirra Willa Pavilion (210–13)
Date: 2013
Location: Somersby, New
South Wales, Australia
Architect: Matthew Woodward
Area: 72m² (775ft²)

**Yeosu Expo Hyundai Motor
Group Pavilion (148–49)**
Date: 2012
Location: Yeosu, South Korea
Architect: UnSangDong
Architects; Jang Yoon Gyoo
and Shin Chang Hoon
Client: Hyundai Motors Group
Area: 2,334m² (25,122ft²)

Youturn Pavilion (100–01)
Date: 2010
Location: São Paulo, Brazil
Architect: UNStudio; Ben
van Berkel
Client: 29th Art Biennale,
Fundação Bienal de São Paulo
Area: 125m² (1,345ft²)

FURTHER READING

Adjaye, David, and Peter Allison, *Adjaye, Africa, Architecture,* London, 2011

Bingham-Hall, Patrick, *Peter Stutchbury – Selected Projects,* Sydney 2010

Birnbaum, Daniel, and Madeleine Grynsztejn, *Olafur Eliasson,* London, 2002

Buntrock, Dana, *Toyo Ito,* London, 2014

Escher, Cornelia, and Megumi Komura, *Atelier Bow-Wow: A Primer,* Cologne, 2013

Frampton, Kenneth, *Kengo Kuma: Complete Works,* London, 2013

Frimbois, Jean-Pierre, *Arne Quinze: Modern Contemporary,* Berlin, 2011

Fujimori Terunobu: Architecture, Tokyo, 2007

Gossel, Peter, and Michael Monninger, *Coop Himmelb(l)au,* Cologne, 2010

Harpa: Henning Larsen Architects and Batteriid Architects in Collaboration with Olafur Eliasson, Berlin, 2013

Heatherwick, Thomas, and Maisie Rowe, *Thomas Heatherwick: Making,* London, 2015

Herzog & De Meuron, 2005–2013, Madrid, 2013

Hrankovic, David (ed.), *Hiroshi Sugimoto: Glass Tea House Mondrian,* Cologne, 2015

Iles, Chrissie, and Bennett Simpson, *Dan Graham: Beyond,* Cambridge, MA, 2009

Jodidio, Philip, *Hadid: Complete Works, 1979–2013,* Cologne, 2013

—, *Shigeru Ban: Complete Works, 1985–2010,* Cologne, 2010

—, and Janet Adams Strong, *I. M. Pei, Complete Works,* New York, 2008

Kaltwasser, Martin, and Folke Kobberling, *Ressource Stadt – City as a Resource: One Man's Trash is Another's Treasure,* Berlin 2006

Lee, Christopher M., et al., *Working in Series: Christopher C. M. Lee and Kapil Gupta/Serie Architects,* London 2010

London, Geoffrey, *Tonkin Zulaikha Greer,* Sydney 2004

Marlow, Tim, and John Tancock, *Ai Weiwei,* London, 2015

Morris, Alison, *John Pawson: Plain Space,* London, 2010

Snøhetta: People, Process, Projects, Oslo, 2015

Sou Fujimoto: Architecture Works, 1995–2015, Tokyo, 2015

Steele, Brett, et al., *Didier Fiuza Faustino: Misarchitectures,* London 2015

Studio Mumbai: Praxis, Japan, 2012

Sudjic, Deyan, *Norman Foster: A Life in Architecture,* New York, 2010

Unsangdong Architects – Compound Body, Florence 2011

UNStudio in Motion, London, 2011

Vindum, Kjeld, *Henning Larsen: The Architect's Studio,* Louisiana 2002

Philip Jodidio is internationally renowned
as one of the most popular writers on
architecture. He is the author of numerous
books, including monographs on Tadao
Ando, Santiago Calatrava, Norman Foster,
Richard Meier, Jean Nouvel and Zaha Hadid,
as well as *The Japanese House Reinvented*
(2015), also published by Thames & Hudson.

INDEX